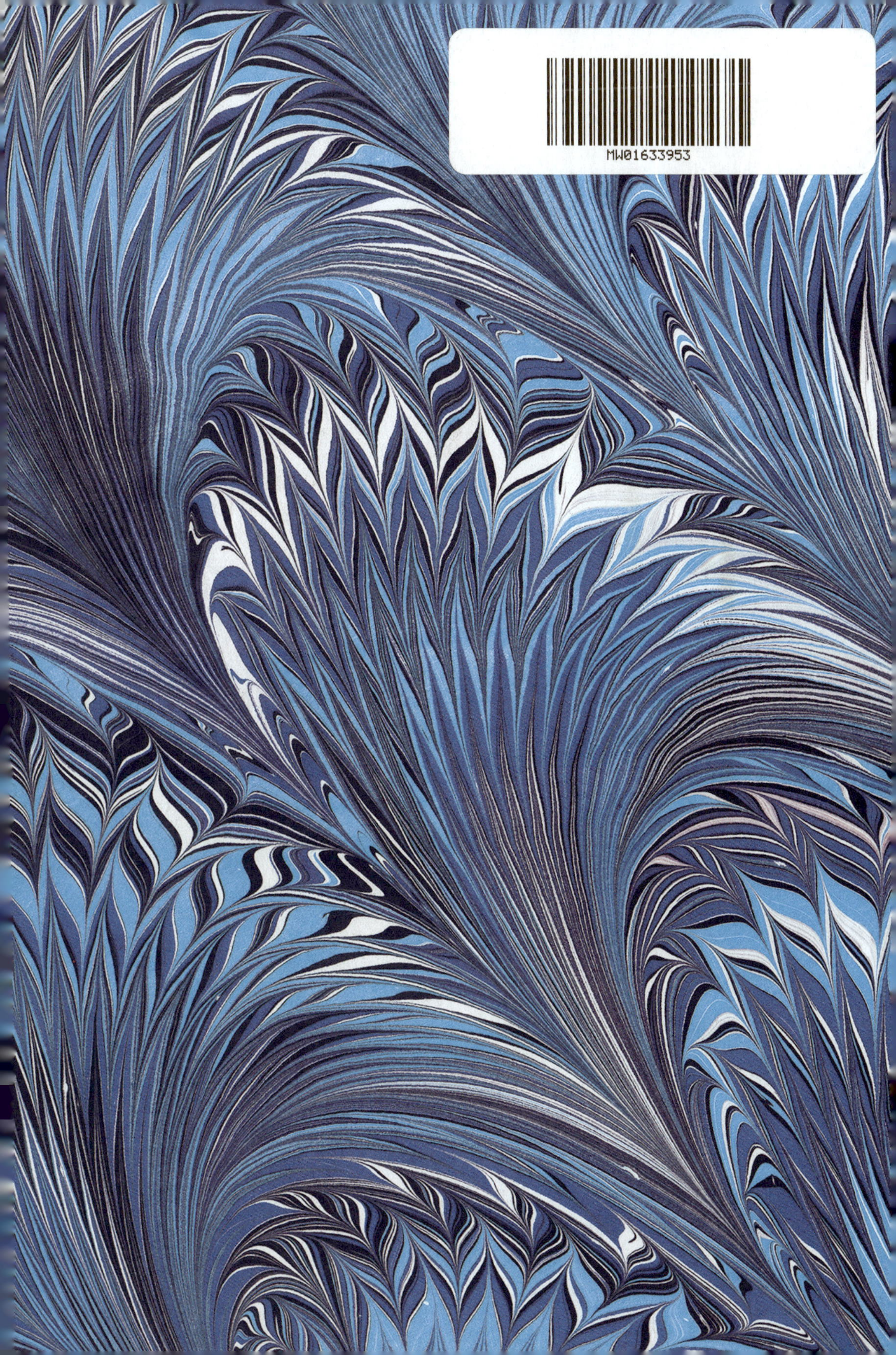
MW01633953

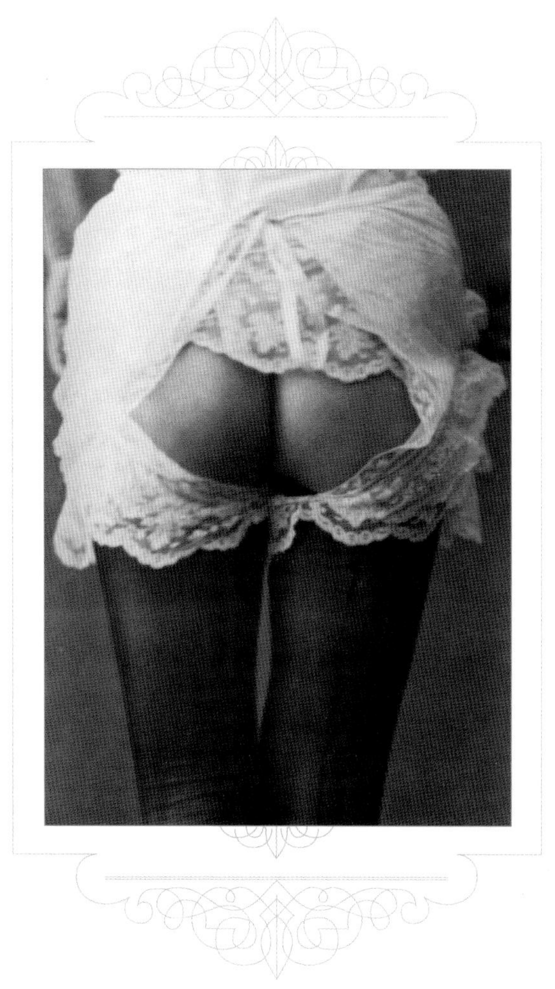

"I bid him come towards me and give me his letter, at the same time throwing down, carelessly, a book I had in my hands. He colour'd, and came within reach of delivering me the letter which he held out, awkwardly enough, for me to take, with his eyes riveted on my bosom, which was, through the design'd disorder of my handkerchief, sufficiently bare, and rather shaded than hid."

Fanny Hill: Memoirs of a Woman of Pleasure

JOHN CLELAND (1749)

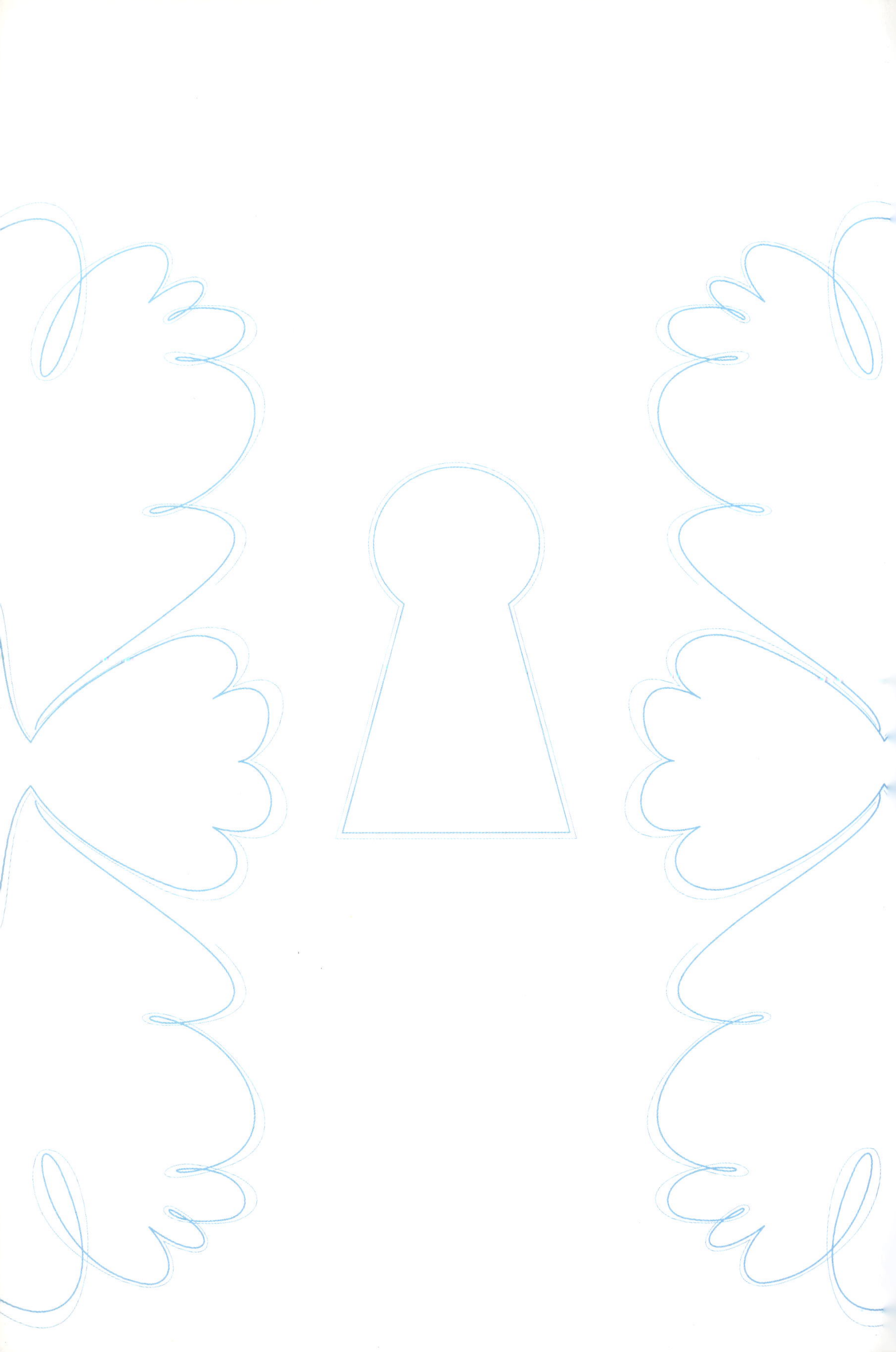

25,000 YEARS ~ OF ~ EROTIC FREEDOM

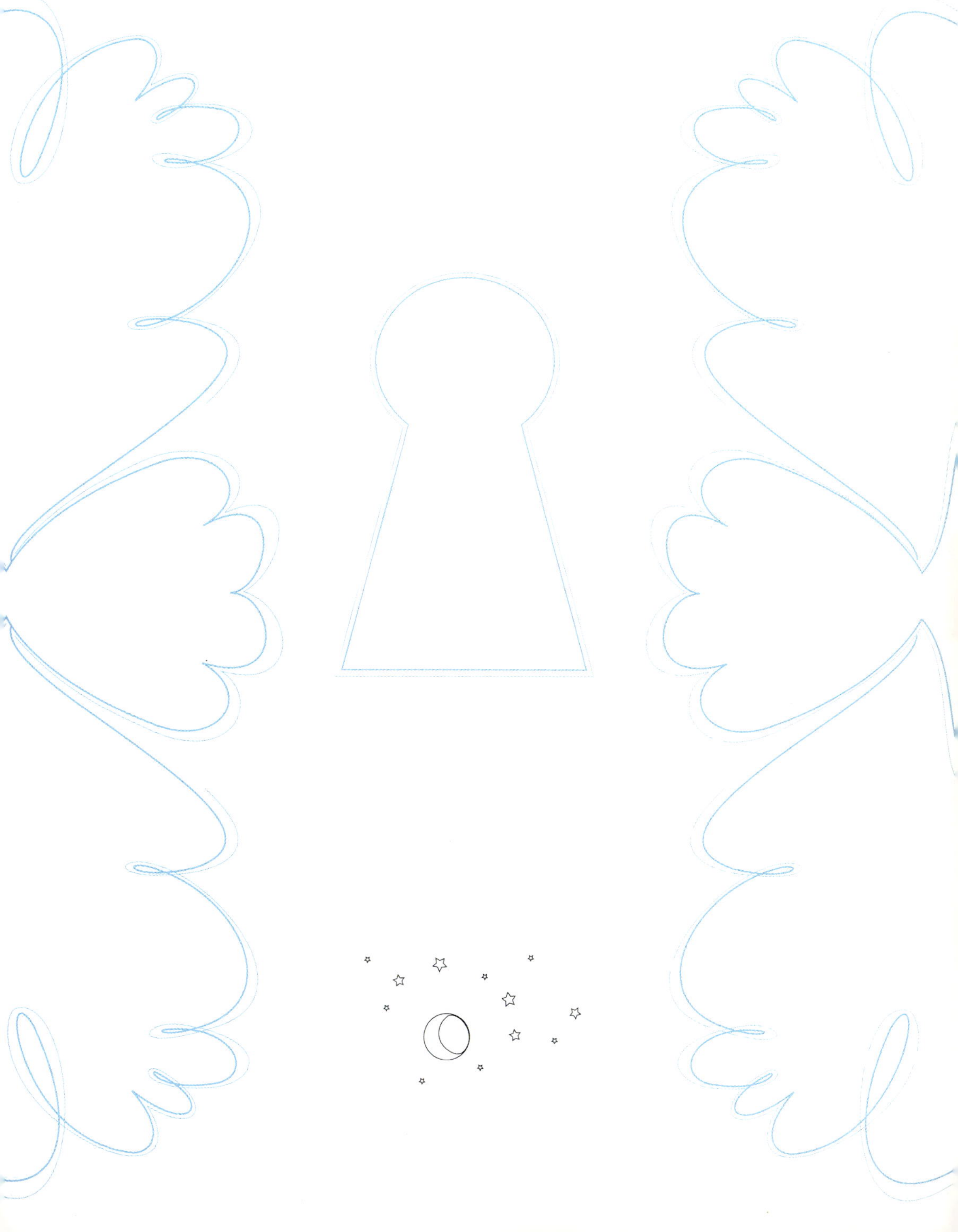

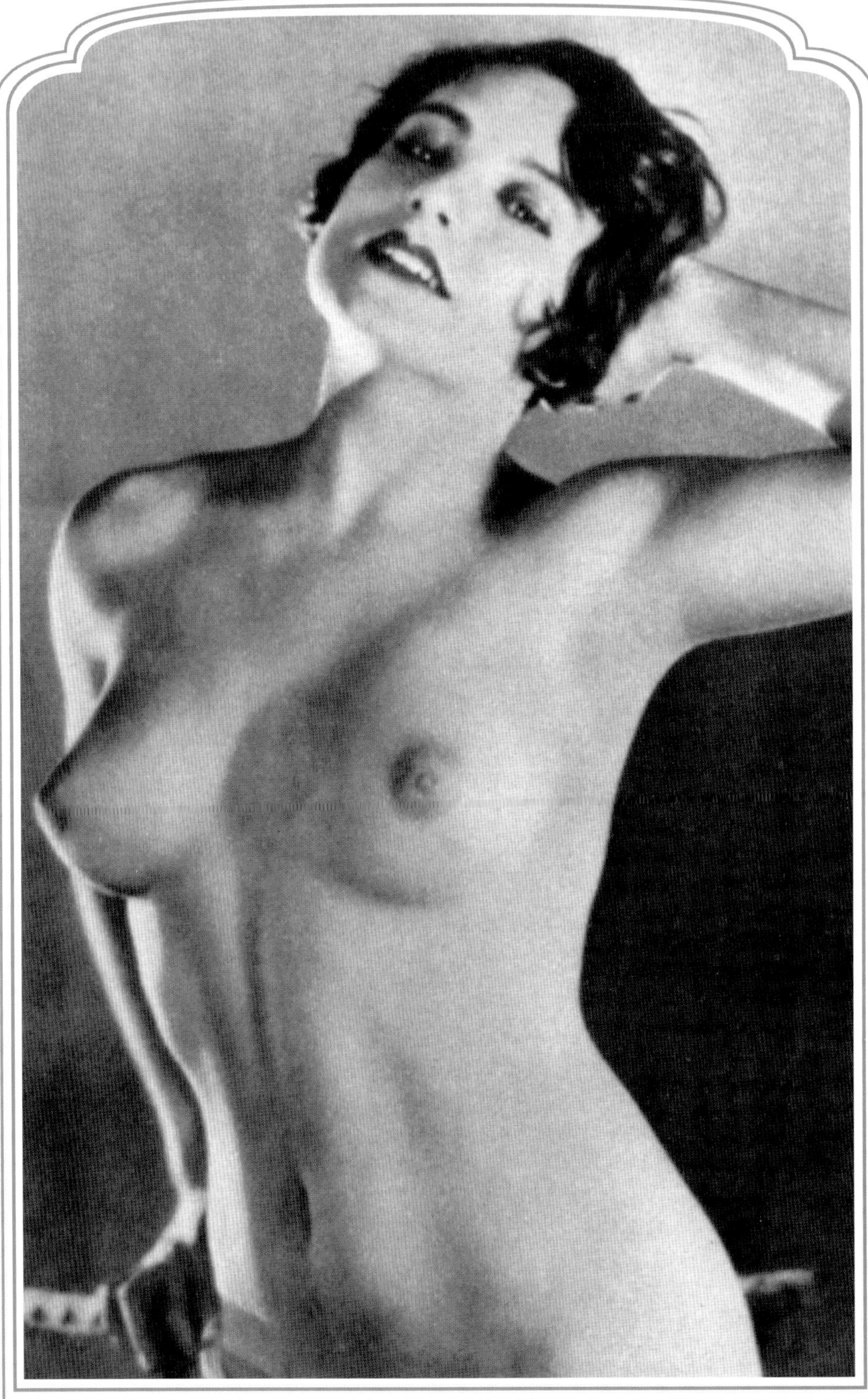

25,000 YEARS

OF

EROTIC FREEDOM

ABRAMS · NEW YORK

25,000

OF EROTIC

VENUS OF WILLENDORF BELIEVED TO HAVE BEEN CREATED BETWEEN 24,000 - 22,000 B.C.

753 B.C. – FOUNDING OF ROME

730 B.C. – FOUNDING OF ITALIAN COLONIES

FIFTH CENTURY B.C. – GREEK ARTISTS CREATED AN INEXHAUSTIBLE CATALOGUE OF PORNOGRAPHIC RENDERINGS OF REVELERS ON THE SURFACE OF THEIR GOBLETS, VASES, AND AMPHORAS.

1147 - 49 – SECOND CRUSADE

1189 - 92 – THIRD CRUSADE

1199 - 1204 – FOURTH CRUSADE

1217 - 21 – FIFTH CRUSADE

1228 - 29 – SIXTH CRUSADE

IN THE MIDDLE AGES HUNDREDS OF EROTIC CARVINGS COULD BE FOUND ON THE COLONNADES OF GOTHIC CHURCHES.

THE RENAISSANCE

1430 - 32 – *DAVID* BY DONATELLO

1480 – *BIRTH OF VENUS* BY SANDRO BOTTICELLI

1559 – POPE PAUL IV SENDS A LIST OF BOOKS THAT HE HAS BANNED TO THE INQUISITION.

1564 – THE COUNCIL OF TRENT OF THE CATHOLIC CHURCH ISSUES THE *INDEX LIBRORUM PROHIBITUM* (INDEX OF PROHIBITED BOOKS). THE INDEX IS UPDATED EVERY FIFTY YEARS UNTIL 1948, EVENTUALLY INCLUDING MORE THAN 4,000 WORKS. THE INDEX WAS RESCINDED IN 1965.

KING GEORGE III ISSUES ROYAL PROCLAMATION OF 1787 "FOR THE ENCOURAGEMENT OF PIETY AND VIRTUE, AND FOR THE PREVENTING OF VICE, PROFANENESS, AND IMMORALITY."

YEARS

F R E E D O M

FIRST CENTURY B.C. – THE ROMANS PRODUCED THE FRESCOES IN THE VILLA DEI MISTERI AT POMPEII AND THE MOSAICS OF NAPLES SAVED FROM THE ASHES OF VESUVIUS—THESE REPRESENT THE MANY SEXUAL VARIATIONS THAT GODS AND HUMANS BROUGHT TO THE SEXUAL ACT.

78 A.D. – DESTRUCTION OF POMPEII

412 - 672 – VISIGOTHS IN SPAIN

489 - 540 – OSTROGOTHS IN ITALY

56 - 774 – LOMBARDS IN ITALY

1027 – TURKISH CONQUEST OF JERUSALEM

1095 – FIRST CRUSADE LAUNCHED

1497 – SAVONAROLA, A NOTORIOUS AND POWERFUL CENSOR, PERSUADED ARTISTS OF FLORENCE TO DESTROY THEIR WORKS–INCLUDING DRAWINGS OF NUDES–IN BONFIRES.

1499 – *DAMNED CAST INTO HELL* BY LUCA SIGNORELLI

1536 - 41 – MICHELANGELO PORTRAYS THE PUNISHMENT OF SODOMY IN THE LAST JUDGMENT ON THE VAULTS OF THE SISTINE CHAPEL.

1542 – POPE PAUL III ESTABLISHES THE UNIVERSAL ROMAN INQUISITION/CONGREGATION OF THE HOLY OFFICE. HIS SACRED DUTIES INCLUDE THE EXAMINATION AND CONDEMNATION OF IMMORAL WORKS OF ART.

LICENSING ACT OF 1662 GIVES THE ENGLISH COURTS A VAGUE MANDATE TO SUPPRESS INDECENT PUBLICATIONS, BUT DOES INDICATE WHAT WOULD BE CONSIDERED “INDECENT.”

“PORNOGRAPHY” COMES INTO WIDESPREAD USE AS A TERM IN THE NINETEENTH CENTURY, APPEARING IN THE OXFORD ENGLISH DICTIONARY IN 1857.

SCANDAL OF OSCAR WILDE’S TRIALS OF 1895

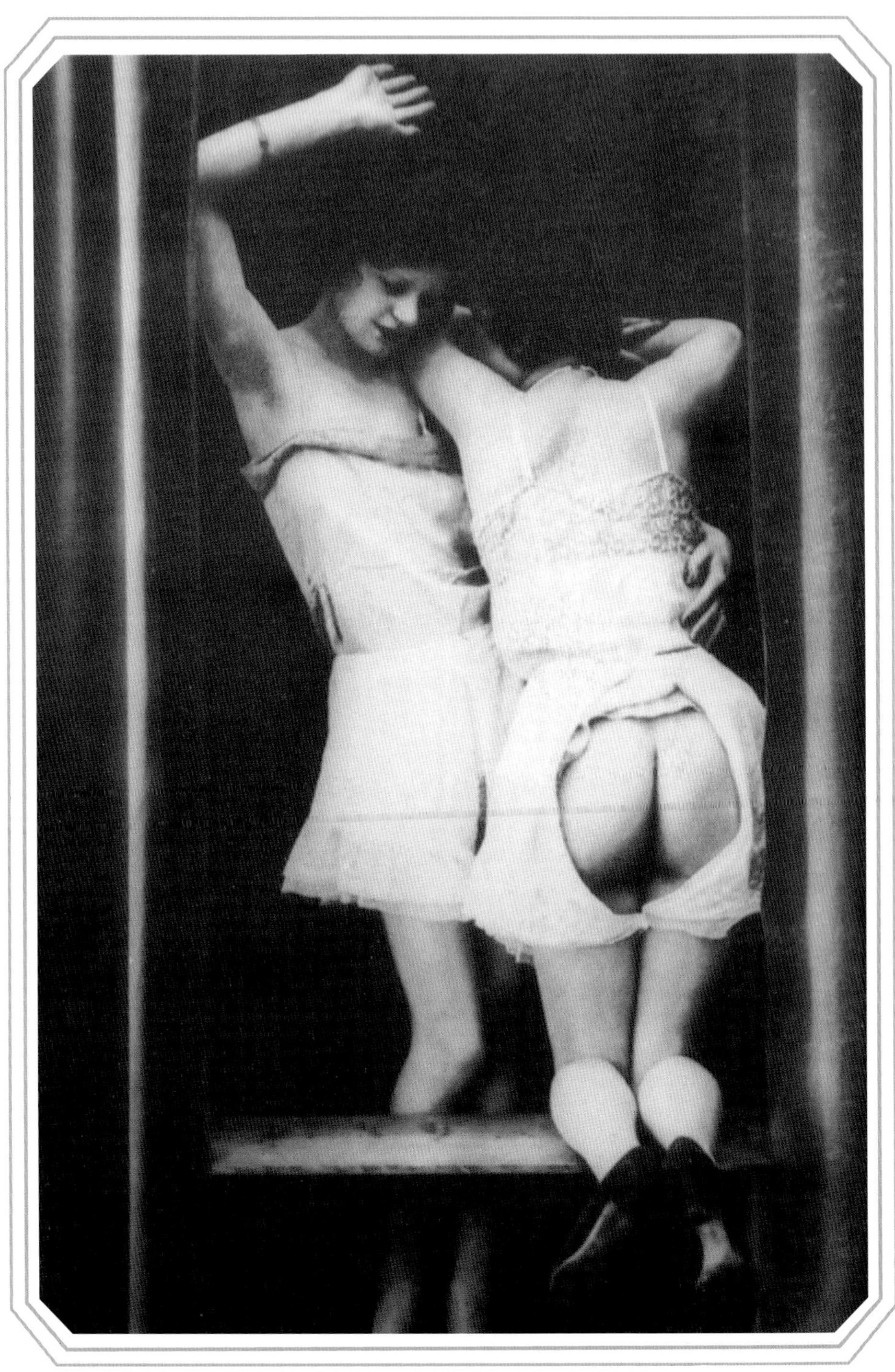

Anonymous VINTAGE DAGUERREOTYPE OF FRENCH *FILLE DE JOIE*, CIRCA 1870

SOME THOUGHTS CONCERNING

PORNOGRAPHY

BY ALAN MOORE

WHETHER WE SPEAK PERSONALLY or palaeoanthropologically, it's fair to say that we humans start out fiddling with ourselves. Our improved scan technology reveals that most of us commence a life of self-pollution while *in utero*, and if we trace our culture back to the first artifacts that showed we had a culture, then we find ourselves confronted by a hubcap-headed humming-top of tits and ass carved lovingly from limestone, excavated from an Aurignacian settlement discovered in a northeastern Austrian village known as Willendorf.

The mighty Robert Crumb, back in his awesomely prolific *Weirdo* days, depicted the creator of the first *Venus of Willendorf* as Caveman Bob, a neurasthenic outcast with a strong resemblance to Crumb himself—perpetually horny, crouching in his cave, and whacking off over the big-butt fetish woman he had just made. *Homo erectus.*

Crumb's point, in all probability, was that while she may well have functioned as a magic icon to induce fertility, and while *to modern eyes she stands as an example of the prehistoric genesis of art,* the Willendorf Venus was an object of arousal in the eyes of her creator, a piece of stone-age stroke material—primal pornography. He may also have been saying that if we trace culture to its very origins, we find its instigator to be an obsessive smut-hound and compulsive masturbator much like Crumb himself—or me, or you, or any of us if we are to be entirely candid.

Humans, whether individually while in the womb or as a species newly climbed down from the treetops that we had shared with kissing-cousin bonobos, discover early on that sexual self-stimulation is a source of great gratification, practically unique in our experience as mammals in that it is easily achievable and, unlike almost every other primitive activity, can be accomplished without risk of being maimed or eaten. Also, it can be acquired completely free of charge, which may well be a factor in society's subsequent attempts to regulate the sexual imagination—a point to which we'll return later.

This is not to say, of course, that all society is a direct result of chronic onanism, although I can see how one might come to that conclusion. Rather, it is to suggest that our impulse toward pornography has been with us since thumbs were first opposable, and that back at the outset of our bipedal experiment we saw it as a natural part of life, one of the nicer parts at that, and as a natural subject for our proto-artists.

Lest this be seen as a reinforcement of the view that porn is wholly a Neanderthal pursuit, we should perhaps consider ancient Greece and the erotic friezes that adorned its civic centers—the magnificently sculpted marble figure of the god Pan violating many of our current barnyard statutes and a really slutty nanny goat in the bargain. Images such as these were clearly seen as eminently suitable Grecian street furniture, depictions of an aspect of mammalian existence that all mammals knew about already and were comfortable regarding, and which no one from the youngest child to the most pious priest needed protecting from. In bygone Greece we see a culture plainly unperturbed by its erotic inclinations, largely saturated by both sexual imagery and sexual narratives.

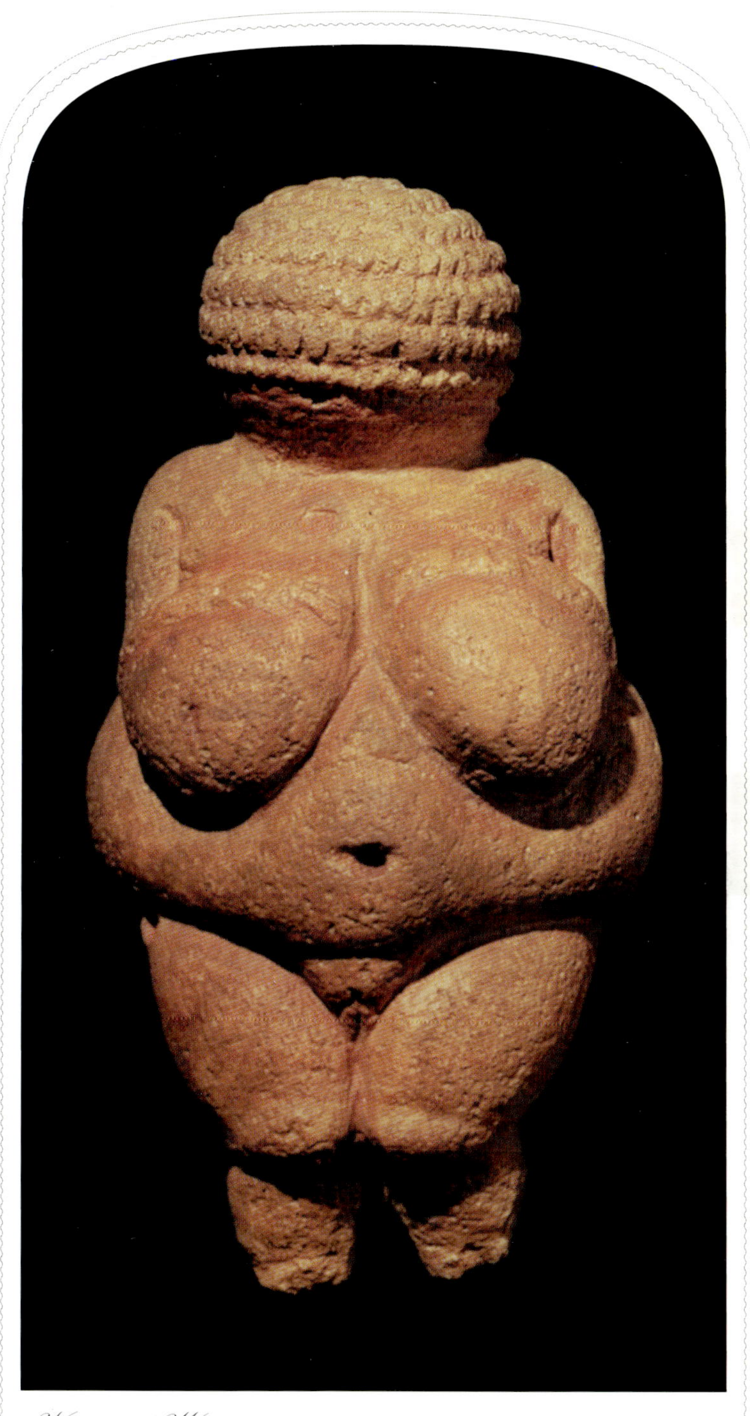

Venus of Willendorf DISCOVERED BY ARCHAEOLOGIST JOSEF SZOMBATHY. CREATED BETWEEN 24,000 B.C. AND 22,000 B.C.

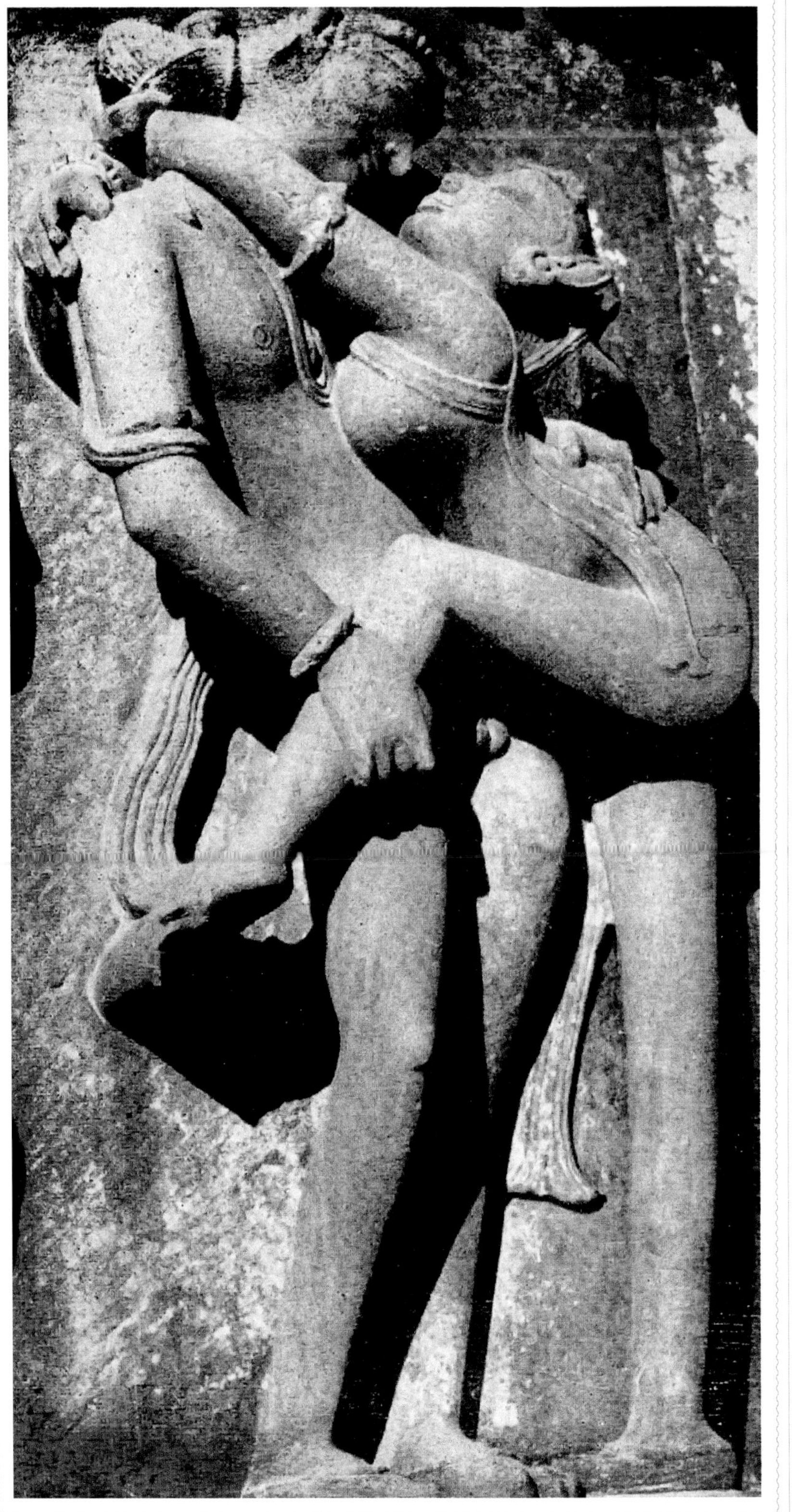

We also see a culture where these attitudes would seem to have worked out quite well, both for the ancient Greeks and for humanity at large. They may well have been hollow-eyed and hairy-palmed erotomaniacs, but on the plus side they invented science, literature, philosophy, and, well, civilization, as it turns out.

Sexual openness and cultural progress walked hand-in-hand throughout the opening chapters of the human story in the West, and it wasn't until the advent of Christianity, or more specifically of the apostle Paul, that anybody realized we should all be thoroughly ashamed of both our bodies and those processes relating to them. Not until the Emperor Constantine had cut and pasted modern Christianity together from loose scraps of Mithraism and the solar cult of Sol Invictus, adopting the resultant theological collage as the religion of the Roman Empire, did we get to witness the effect of its ideas and doctrines when enacted on a whole society.

If we take a traditional (and predominantly Christian) view of the collapse of Rome, then conventional wisdom tells us that Rome was destroyed by decadence, sunk beneath the rising scumline of its orgies and of its own sexual permissiveness. The merest skim through Gibbon, on the other hand, will demonstrate that Rome had been a heaving, decadent, and orgiastic fleshpot more or less since its inception. It had fornicated its way quite successfully through several centuries without showing any serious signs of harm as a result. Once Constantine introduced compulsory Christianity to the Empire, though, it barely lasted another hundred years.

Largely, this was because Rome relied on foreign troops—on cavalry from Egypt, for example—to defend the Empire against the Teutonic hordes surrounding it. Foreign soldiers were originally happy to enlist, since Rome at that point took a pagan and syncretic standpoint that allowed recruits to worship their own gods while they were off in northern Europe holding back the Huns. Once the Empire had been Christianized, however, that was not an option. Rome's new Christian leaders decided that it was their way or the stairway, and so consequently, off in distant lands, recruitment figures plummeted. The next thing anybody knew, there were

Eastern Carvings EROTIC CARVINGS ON THE DEVI JAGADAMBI TEMPLE BUILT BY THE RULERS OF THE CHANDELLA DYNASTY BETWEEN THE TENTH AND TWELFTH CENTURIES

barbarians everywhere: the Huns, the Franks, the Visigoths, and worst of all the Goths, with their white contact lenses and Cradle of Filth collections. Rome, effectively, was over, bar the shouting.

So, to recap what we have learned so far: Sexually open and progressive cultures such as ancient Greece have given the West almost all of its civilizing aspects, whereas sexually repressive cultures such as late Rome have given us the Dark Ages.

Let us fast-forward past almost a thousand years of Saxons, Danes, and Vikings ripped on fly agaric pillaging and raping their way through some sort of meteoric nuclear winter with brains dripping from their axes, howling about Odin and blood-eagling anybody who chose not to do the same. When lights eventually started to come on again across the Western world, we find a Christian church that's understandably concerned about attracting worshippers to its rough-hewn pews—and that had hit upon the notion of erotic art as one way of accomplishing this end. The spread-legged figure with a splayed vagina found crouched in the masonry of many medieval British churches, misidentified as a Sheelagh-na-Gig, as a leftover mother-goddess from some earlier religion, was in fact of purely Christian origin and was originally intended as an image representing Lust. If the folklorists had looked harder then they would have almost certainly found similar depictions of Wrath, Gluttony, Sloth, Avarice, and all the other deadly sins, although that petrified and gaping pussy does tend to seize more than its fair share of the attention, which is probably no accident. In churches of that period, displays of pornographic imagery were not at all uncommon, nor were they by any stretch of the imagination unintentional. Pictures of people copulating were a big draw when it came to pulling in the congregations, after all, and were not sinful in themselves if they could be explained away as warnings to the faithful: stern moral instructions to describe the shameful acts that, were they actually committed, would result in certain hellfire and damnation.

What the church actually accomplished with this crowd-pleasing maneuver was a subtle and yet massively important change in the

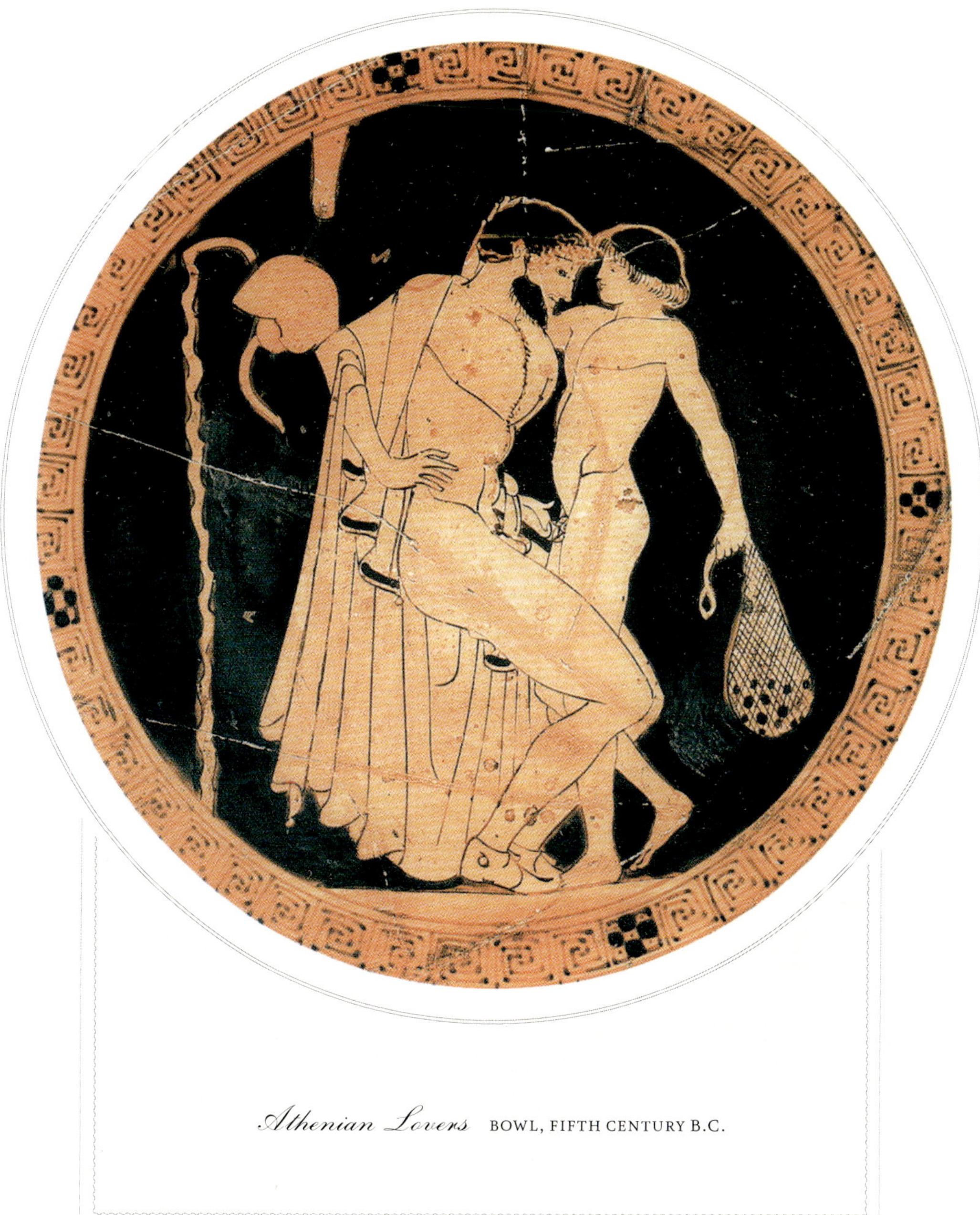

Athenian Lovers BOWL, FIFTH CENTURY B.C.

relationship between the population and its sexual imagination. Implicitly, it was acceptable to enjoy sexual imagery as long as you accepted also that such acts were sinful and felt suitably ashamed and guilty if you were in any way aroused by their depiction. This established the immediate link between the perusal of pornography and intense self-loathing or embarrassment, which still exists today throughout most of the Western world.

It wasn't just the early church, of course, that enjoyed a monopoly on images of naked flesh. Until the nineteenth century, the only way an artist could portray the unclothed body without risk of censure was to set the nudes within a context that was either classical or biblical—Eve and the serpent, Leda and the swan—so long as you can't actually see it going in. Mind you, that's not to say that there weren't always artists who were unafraid of censure, or that the church's standpoint on the issue was at all times and in all lands universally observed. The flow of English literature since its Saxon beginnings would seem largely unconcerned with sexual propriety. A few of Chaucer's *Canterbury Tales* are indistinguishable from the soft-core sex romps that swamped English cinemas during the 1970s. *Carry on up the Fourteenth Century. Confessions of a Pardoner.* Shakespeare could work encrypted lavatorial filth into descriptions of a lady's handwriting: "Her Cs, her Us 'N' her Ts, whereby she maketh her great Ps." That said, it wasn't until William Caxton devised his printing press—for younger readers, just think fifteenth-century Internet—that a tradition of pornography as we would understand the term today was able to develop. Just as with the Internet, the new technology was put almost immediately to the purpose of disseminating dirty pictures.

Prior to this point, when mass production first became a possibility, erotic culture had existed only in the private realm of artists and collectors, which in public terms is much the same as saying it did not exist at all. The church had never previously adopted a position on pornography, simply because there wasn't any, and it was relatively slow to recognize it when it finally showed up. By William Blake's day in the last half of the eighteenth century, contemporary London was awash with fuck-books and salacious prints of all varieties, including such essential publications as a best-selling directory of whores that introduced the phrase "as lewd as goats and monkeys" to the English language, meant apparently as a recommendation, as a Regency equivalent to Michelin's four stars. It's also worth remembering the late 1700s as the era during which, in France, the Marquis Donatien Alphonse François de Sade began to use outrageous, violent, scatological, and frequently intensely dull pornography for the first time as a blunt instrument for social satire, finding in society's great squeamishness about its carnal impulses a vulnerable underbelly open to attack.

Yet when the nineteenth century began to get seriously under way, amid European worries with regard to all the revolutions of the previous fifty years coupled with the uncertainty and paranoia typifying the Napoleonic Wars, a more repressive and authoritarian mood prevailed. While an undeniably large number of licentious chapbooks circulated throughout this period, these were already starting to adopt the furtive underground associations and hunched posture that would stigmatize and lame pornography for the next hundred years or so.

As for open involvement in erotic work by writers, artists, or any creators of proven ability, the ground appears to have become a toxic wasteland, poisonous to the reputation and alive with career pathogens. When William Blake expired in 1827, even though his willingness to embrace sexuality and a broad range of sexually unorthodox ideas was central to his whole philosophy, overprotective devotees persuaded his wife, Catherine, to purge his work of any overtly erotic art or writings. That Blake had a love and also a facility for pornographic images can still be seen in his surviving marginalia, with doodled youths gobbled by fleshy matrons, but his acolytes had evidently made their minds up that the poet-visionary they were in the process of constructing would be more angelic without genitalia. We can but imagine, wistfully, the masturbatory masterworks incinerated in Blake's bonfire of profanities—*The Red Dragon Does the Woman Clothed in the Sun*—and it's better that we don't torment ourselves with all the other glorious artists whose posthumous conflagrations, real porno for pyros, may have gone completely unrecorded.

With the guilty and embarrassed tone thus set for the impending reign of Queen Victoria, we find pornography in the condition that has by and large defined it ever since: a wretched ghetto with which no respected artist would desire to be associated, and which therefore rapidly becomes the province of those with no literary or artistic leanings whatsoever. The once rich erotic landscape was effectively deserted by the genuinely talented. It turned eventually into a genre that not only had no standards but also appeared to think it had no need of them, although during Victorian times this total desertification was still some way off into the future, and the cultural libido was still showing healthy spurts of life from time to time.

Indeed, the façade of abstemious morality that came as part of the Victorian packaging appeared to reproduce hot-house conditions in the prurient imagination of the day. Pornography, exemplified by periodicals such as *The Pearl,* could flourish, albeit only as an underground subculture. This subterranean network, though, extended a considerable way beneath surface society, so that the semi-detached homesteads of Victorian suburbia were dangerously undermined. In those times, long before the advent of the adult video outlet, city businessmen returning homeward for a weekend with their spouse or partner would call in at some backstreet establishment and pick up a gaslight equivalent: just as theater predates cinema, so too did fully scored dramatic home pornography precede the skin-flick. Pornographic playlets could be purchased, ranging from two-person dramas through to full ensemble pieces if the neighbors were agreeable. These publications came with sheet music, so that if one of the participants were musically inclined then he or she could sit at the piano and provide a vigorous accompaniment to whatever activity was taking place upon the hearth rug or the horsehair sofa. (Yes, I know it sounds ridiculous, but I was told that by Malcolm McLaren, and if you can't trust Malcolm McLaren then whom can you trust?)

Pan and Daphnis ROMAN MARBLE COPY OF A GREEK ORIGINAL FROM THE THIRD AND SECOND CENTURIES BY HELIODOROS, FOUND AT POMPEII

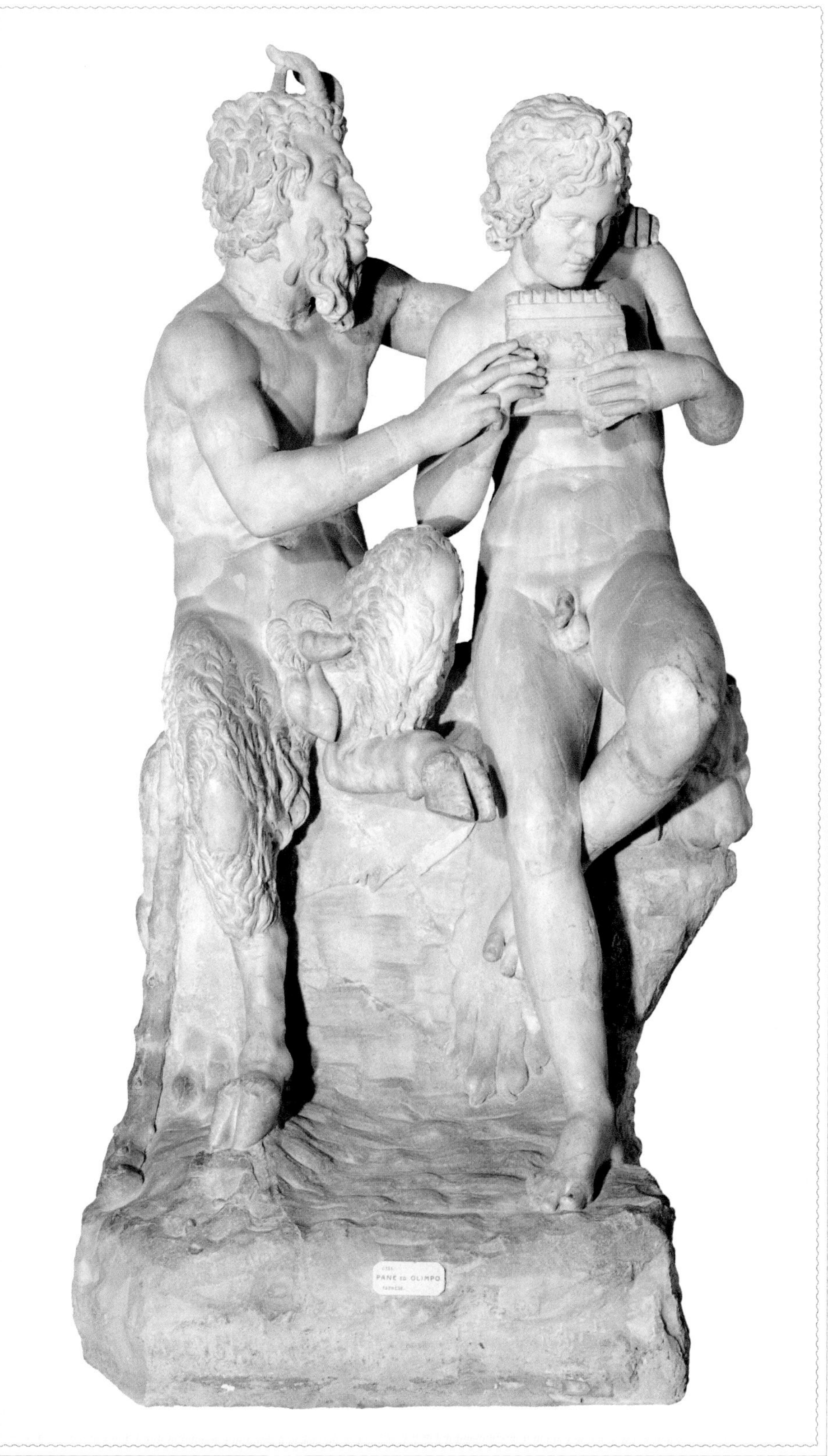
PANE ED OLIMPO

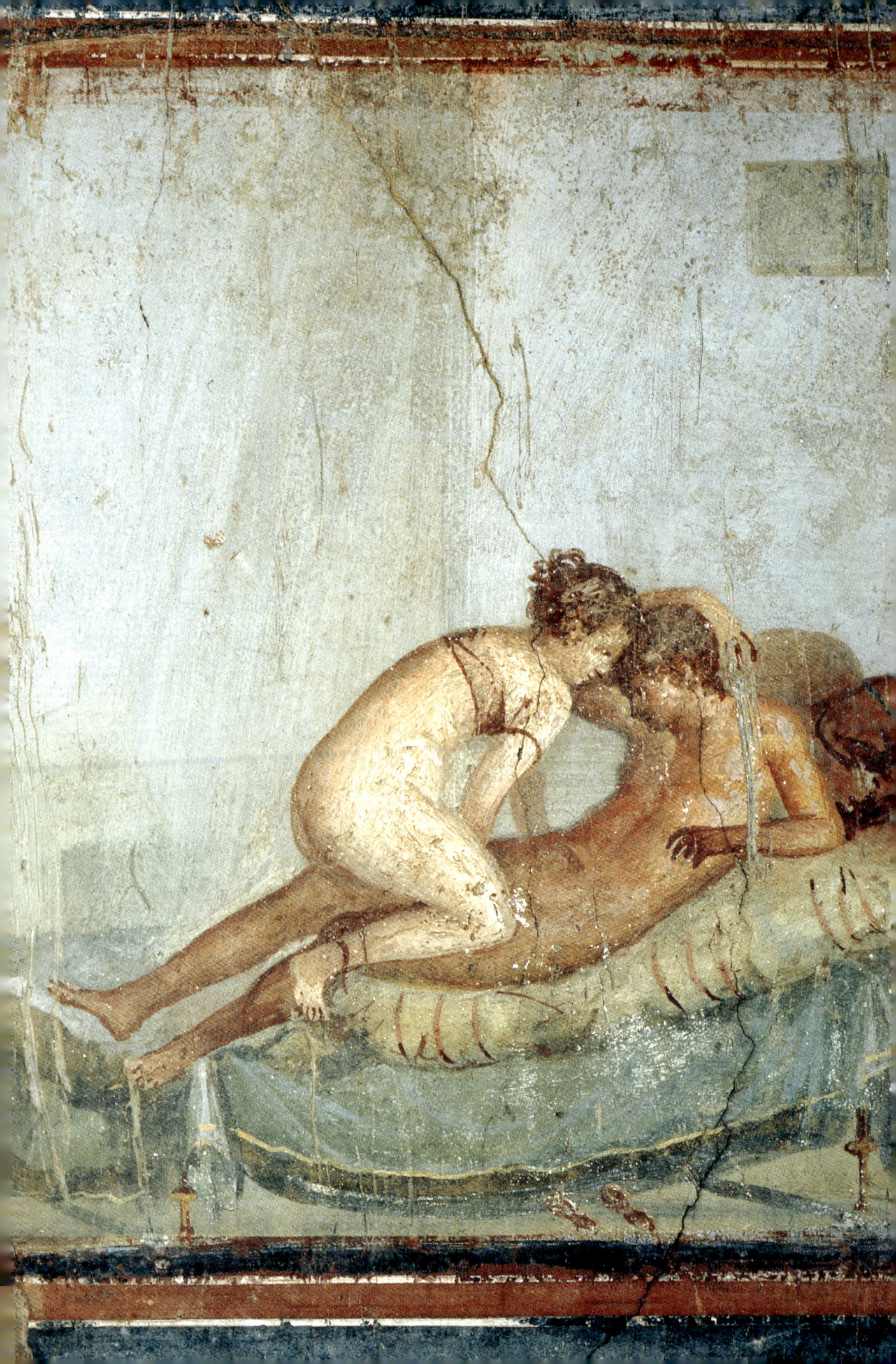

The powerful erotic undercurrent that existed in society behind closed doors, however, was in direct opposition to the era's outward stance on sexual matters, and increasingly pornography was openly deplored as an unpardonable affront to public virtue. One collector of erotica, with many scurrilous unpublished manuscripts by Swinburne, Wilde, and other notables, had been warned by his lady wife that, on his death, she was intent upon incinerating the entire obscene collection. Cunningly, the gentleman in question got around this by persuading the British Museum to accept a "private case" containing his salacious valuables, a trick he only managed to pull off by making the safekeeping of his titillating treasures a condition of the museum also getting all his first editions of Cervantes.

In the middle of the nineteenth century, of course, photography became an option for pornographers, though this was a development that introduced a new (and later vastly controversial) element to the erotic, or at least to the moral debate concerning it: These images were not the fruit of an aroused imagination, but were actual people who had lives beyond the photographic cropping of the dirty postcard that contained them. Concern for the models' moral well-being would come to equal or surpass concern for the impressionable members of the public who might be exposed to the material's depraving influence. Back in those early days, though, when a camera was a relatively rare possession, at least in comparison with the notepad and pencil that one needed for more low-tech smut, the dominant mode of pornography was literary, and saucy snapshots were at first a fairly rarefied minority concern.

The literary mainstream of under-the-counter reading matter during the Victorian period varied widely in palatability, as is to be expected in an outcast and despised field without quality control of any kind. A Sadeian passion for deflowering or else for uncritically depicted rape intruded nastily into some narratives, possibly even into a majority, but it's important that we do not overlook the socially benevolent material that found its only outlet in this much-loathed form. Sexual etiquette, and even to a certain extent

Pompeii FRESCO FROM THE VILLA OF CENTENARY IN POMPEII, 1 A.D.

sexual politics, could not be mentioned or discussed within the confines of Victorian propriety, which meant that only in a field already banished far beyond those confines could such subjects safely be brought up. It's by no means unusual to find participants in some chapter-length orgy of the period suddenly declaring half-time during which they will discuss such issues as the gentleman's responsibility to make sure that his female partner has been fully satisfied by their exchange, or the importance of always acceding to the female partner's wishes even when deranged by passion. These were matters that could not be raised in *Home Hints* and were certainly not taught at school or by one's parents. It would seem that the only sexual education being circulated in the nineteenth century was within publications that were by their very definition deemed obscene.

To illustrate this practice we need look no further than the riotous career of local nineteenth-century atheist and member of Parliament Charles Bradlaugh, whose indignant statue stands pointing accusingly upon a traffic island on Abington Square here in Northampton, England. Amid the stream of principled activities and often controversial incidents that marked the life of this confirmed Old Labour politician is a spell in which Bradlaugh was jailed, along with noted Match-Girl agitator and Theosophist, Miss Annie Besant, for the distribution of "obscene material." This turns out to have been advice on contraception, meant for women of the working classes at a time when nearly a third of them might reasonably expect to die in childbirth. Pretty racy stuff, as you can probably imagine.

This intense and largely indiscriminate repression marking the Victorian era, though it was not unopposed and though in many ways it may have even made the period's porno more inventively subversive, could be seen as having triumphed in the end. The victory was Pyrrhic and short-lived, admittedly, with the excesses of the twentieth century poised in the wings and just about to make their lurid entrance, but for those artists caught dabbling in erotic waters when the clampdown came, it must have still seemed a decisive one. While there were obviously a wide variety of complex

Giorgione OVERLEAF: *THE SLEEPING VENUS*, 1508–10

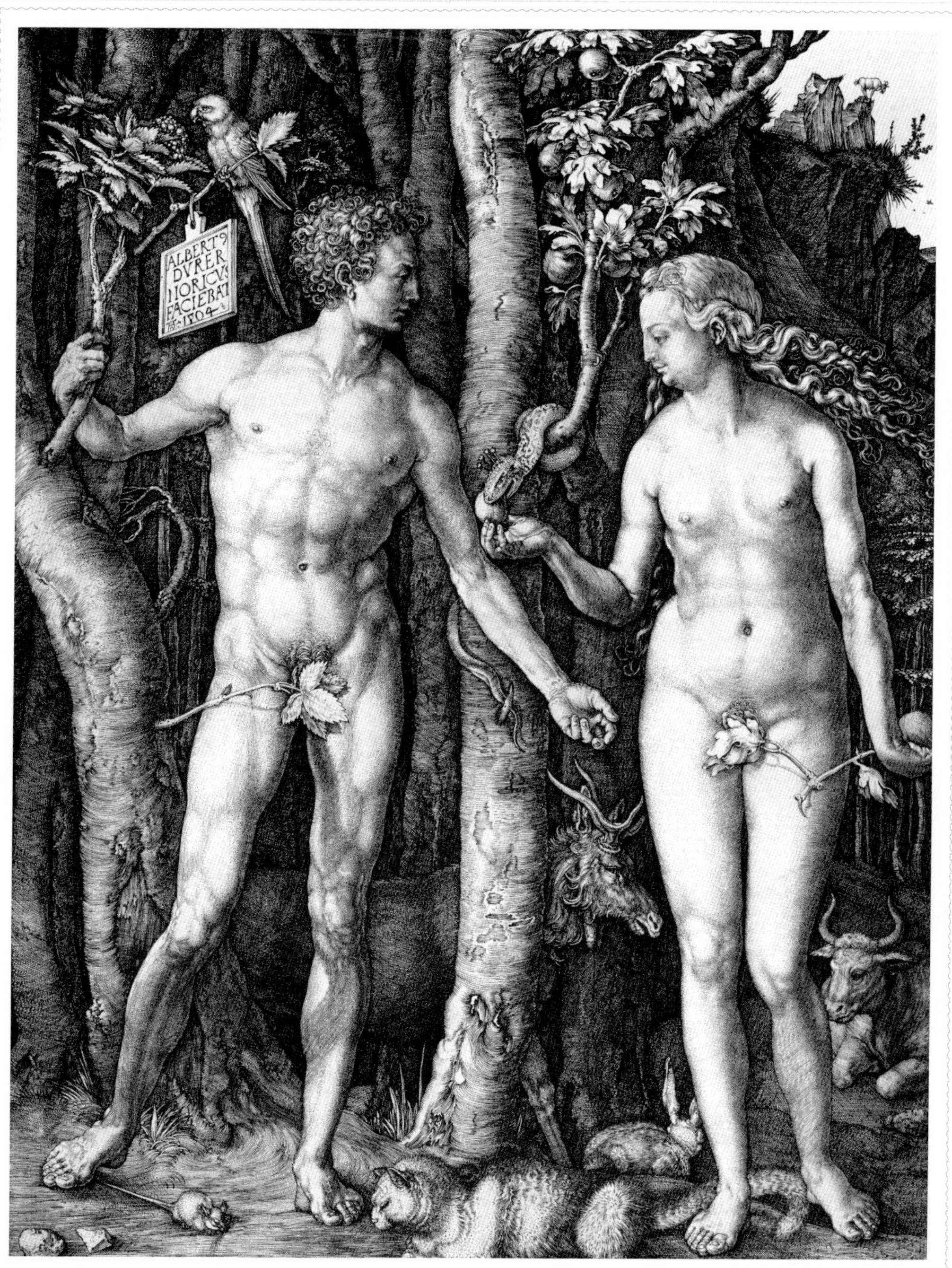

Albrecht Dürer *ADAM AND EVE*, ENGRAVING FROM 1504

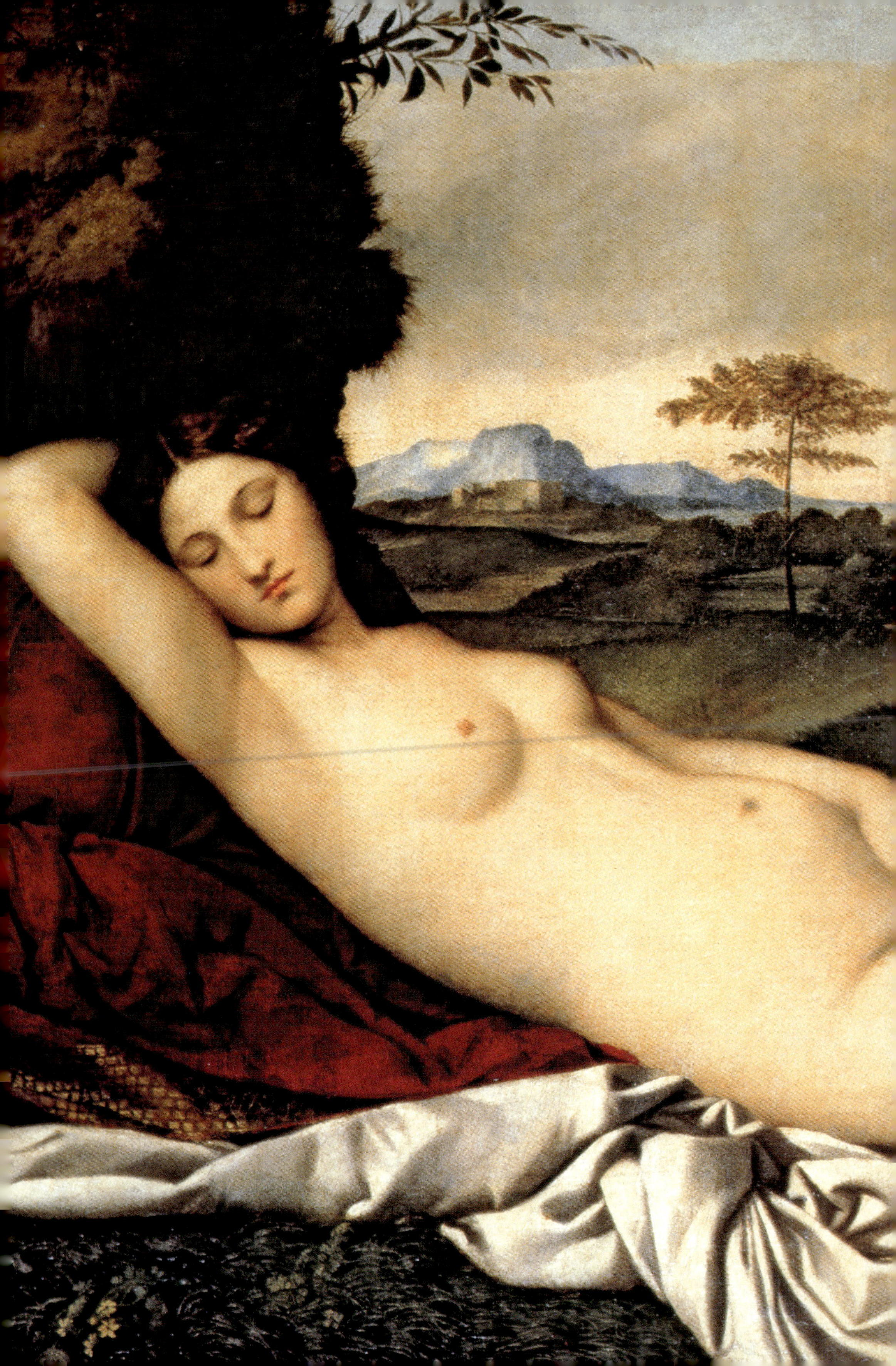

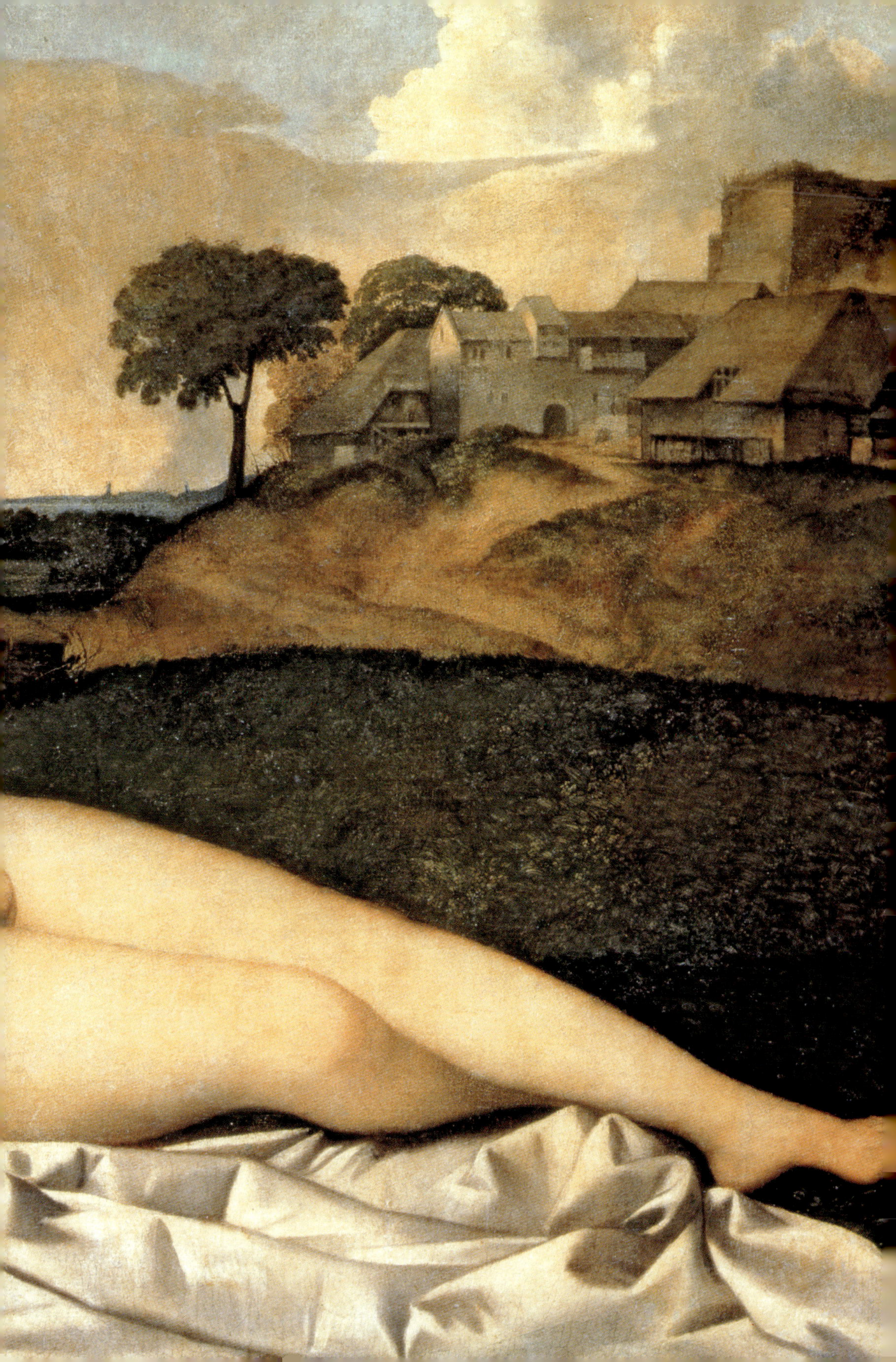

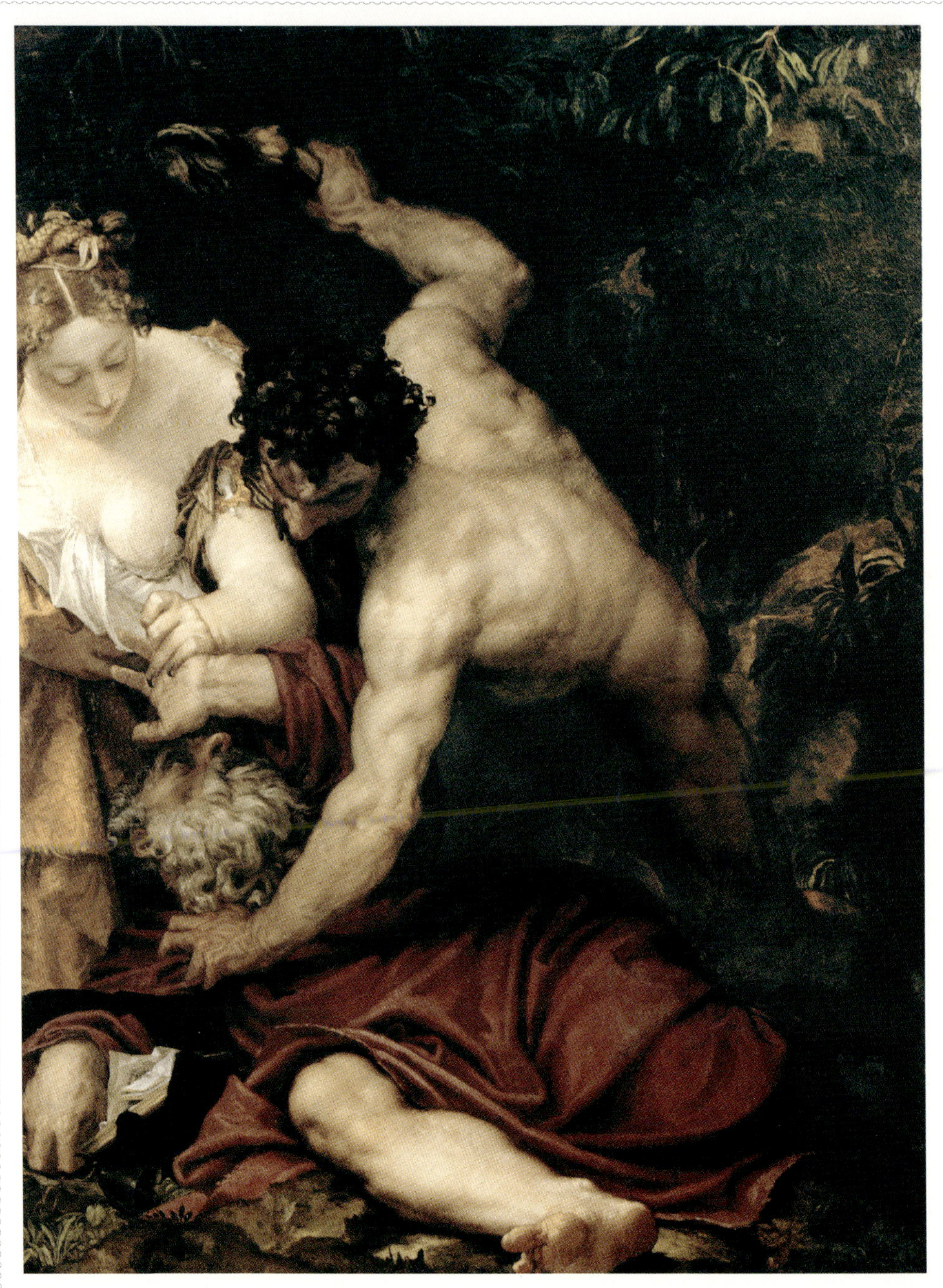

Veronese (Paolo Caliari) *THE TEMPTATION OF ST. ANTHONY*, CIRCA 1552

incidents and issues influencing how affairs progressed around this time, the one event that is most emblematic of this sea-change in the public attitude toward erotica must surely be the trial of Oscar Wilde.

What makes Wilde's downfall so important is the way in which this marvelously gifted aesthete and writer had become a living symbol of the Decadence, the movement that perfumed practically all the important art or literature composed between the 1870s and 1890s. The aesthetics of the movement, as defined by early decadent Theophile Gautier, demand that artists should be unafraid to plunder from the opulence of history or legend for their imagery, and equally feel free to borrow from the latest offerings of their culture—from its "technical vocabularies." Given that the remit of the Decadence was intentionally broad, it's hardly a surprise that the erotic should become a major element informing the whole atmosphere that surrounded the movement. For the first time in a century, genuine artists were again engaging openly and meaningfully with sexual expression in their work, and the exquisite peacock display that resulted must have seemed, in sexually color-blind Victorian eyes, like a red rag to a bull. Even the decorative border lines characterizing Art Nouveau were heavy with the curve and sag of breasts or testicles, even upon those relatively rare occasions when there were no breasts or testicles depicted in the actual illustration.

Literature witnessed a plethora of stellar talents more than willing to apply themselves to the erotic, from the rich and sensual undertones found in the work of J. K. Huysmans to the full-blown pornographic writings of Guillaume Apollinaire or Pierre Louÿs. Louÿs presents an interesting case in that here was a writer blessed with independent means whose work received tremendous critical acclaim quite early on in his career, after *The Love Song of Bilitis* had been published, and yet who found literary fame repulsive and elected to write brilliantly demented hard-core filth for the remainder of his life, safe in the knowledge that it was unpublishable outside the small market in privately printed chapbooks for the connoisseur.

Michelangelo OVERLEAF: *LEDA AND THE SWAN*, ENGRAVING CIRCA 1530

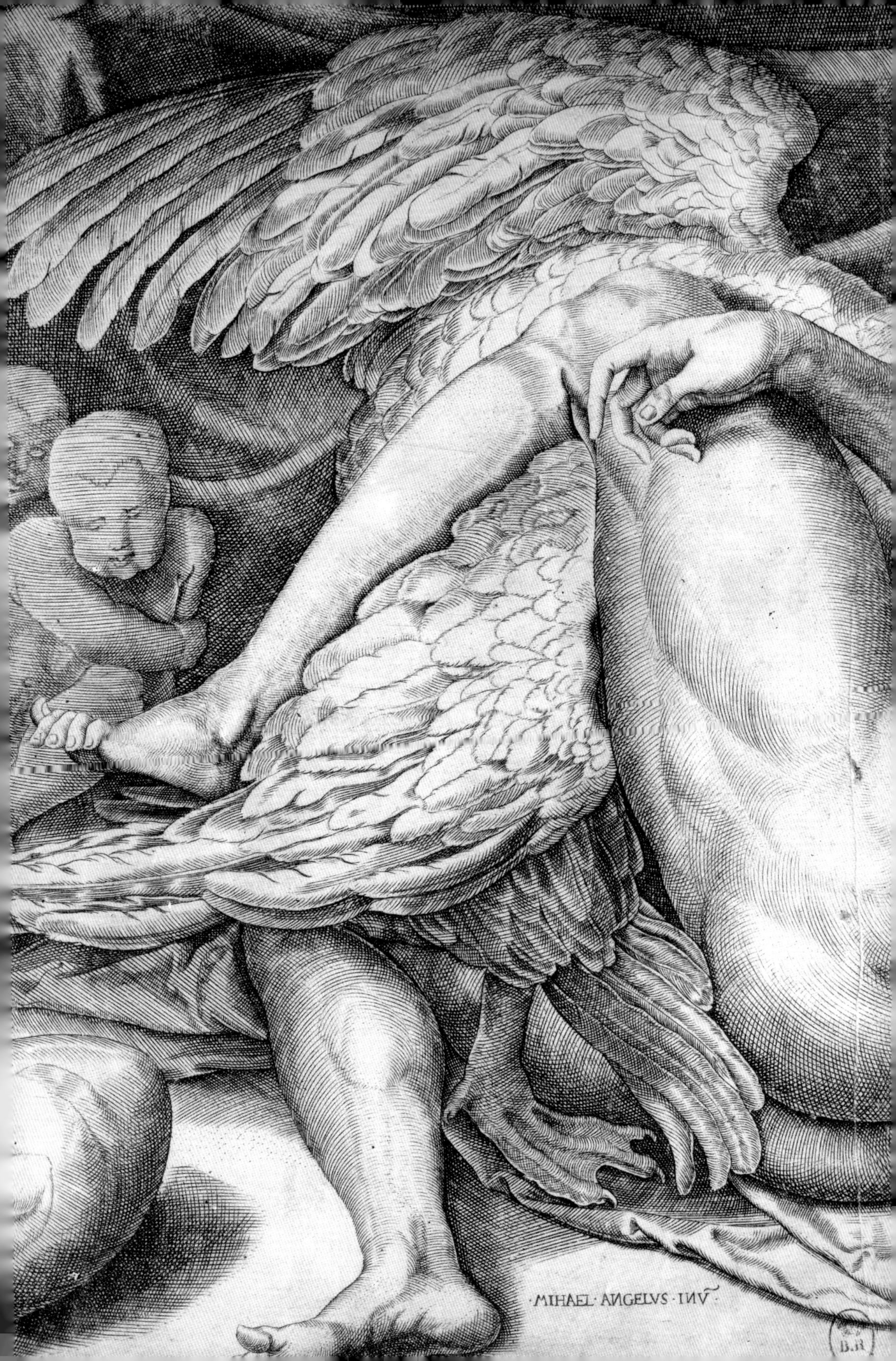
·MIHAEL·ANGELVS·INV

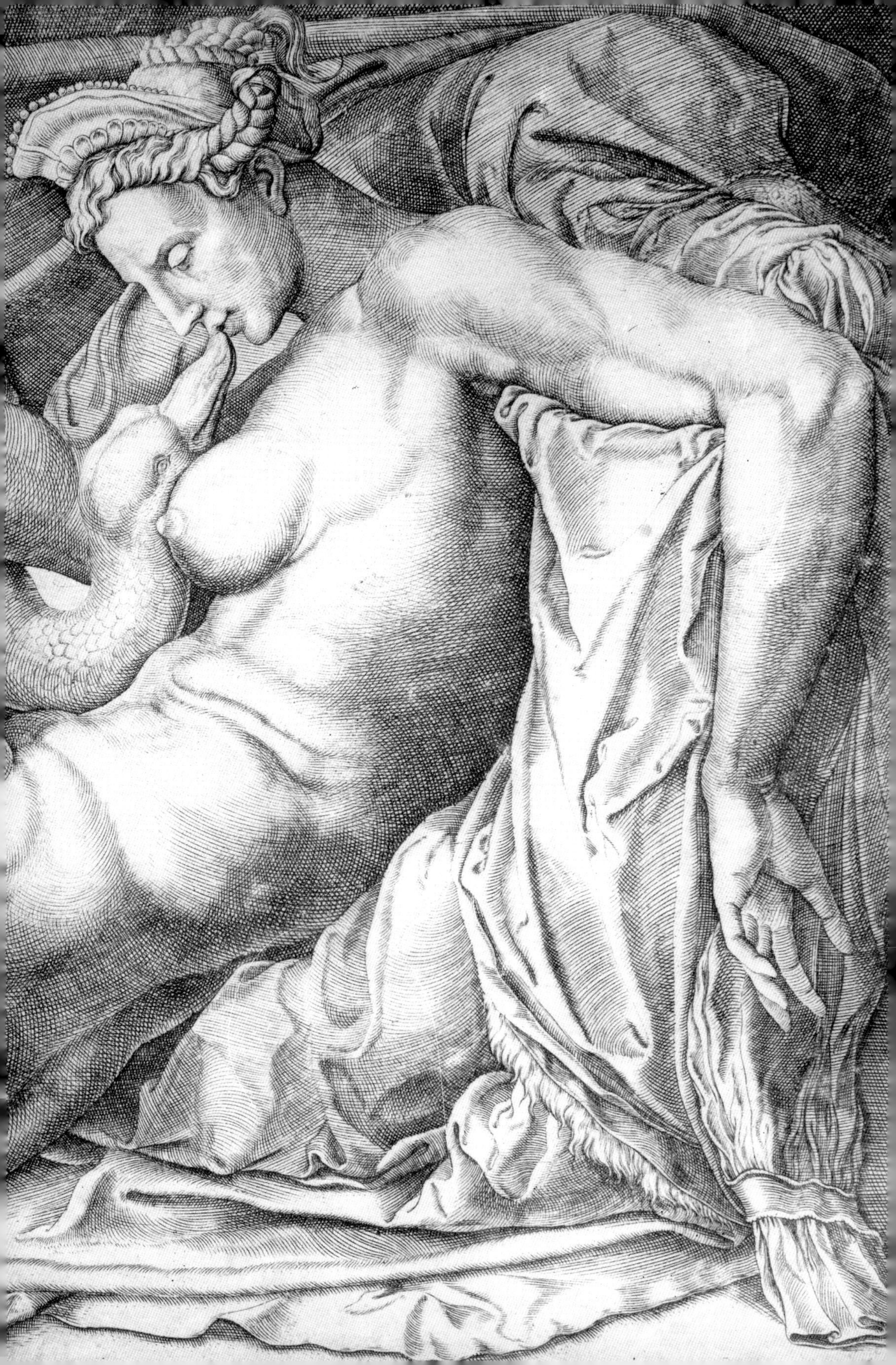

Poetry too was graced during this period with many sublime talents who possessed an ear for the erotic, notably the tragic Ernest Dowson. Dowson, killing himself with his fondness for the green destroyer, absinthe, and besotted with a fifteen-year-old girl, died much too young in relative obscurity after enriching English phraseology with such well-known expressions as "I have been faithful to you, in my fashion," "days of wine and roses," and "gone with the wind." Yes, that was Dowson.

Within visual media, however, and despite fierce competition from the likes of Alphonse Mucha, it is fragile Aubrey Beardsley who emerges as the poster child for sexual expression in the arts during the Decadence. Dead by the age of twenty-six from galloping tuberculosis, Beardsley was, both in his artistry and personal appearance, a rare orchid who would not survive the bitter, disapproving moral blizzards of what William Blake had once referred to as "the English Winter." Although Beardsley's personal life appears, much like Beardsley himself, to be asexual (and despite the fact that save for scurrilous suggestions from Frank Harris of a sexual relationship with his beloved sister Mabel Beardsley, there's no evidence that Aubrey ever physically had intercourse with anyone) the artist's drawings are alive with sexuality. Perhaps, as with the virgin architect Antonio Gaudí, Beardsley's one real form of sexual expression is to be found in his sensual and yearning line.

In a career that spanned no more than eight years, Beardsley's striking style impressed itself upon the public's consciousness through illustrated works such as Sir Thomas Malory's *Morte D'Arthur* or by means of Beardsley's elegant and sinister submissions to John Lane's *Yellow Book.* Although the artist's name became a byword for peculiarity—"Awfully Weirdsley," as one wag rechristened him—the impact of his work, with its tumescent dwarves and aching sexuality, was such that it established Beardsley and his swooping line as the defining spirit of the 1890s. The handful of images that he supplied for Wilde's *Salomé* are among his very best work, although at the same time these are the few illustrations that undoubtedly contributed the most to Beardsley's ruin.

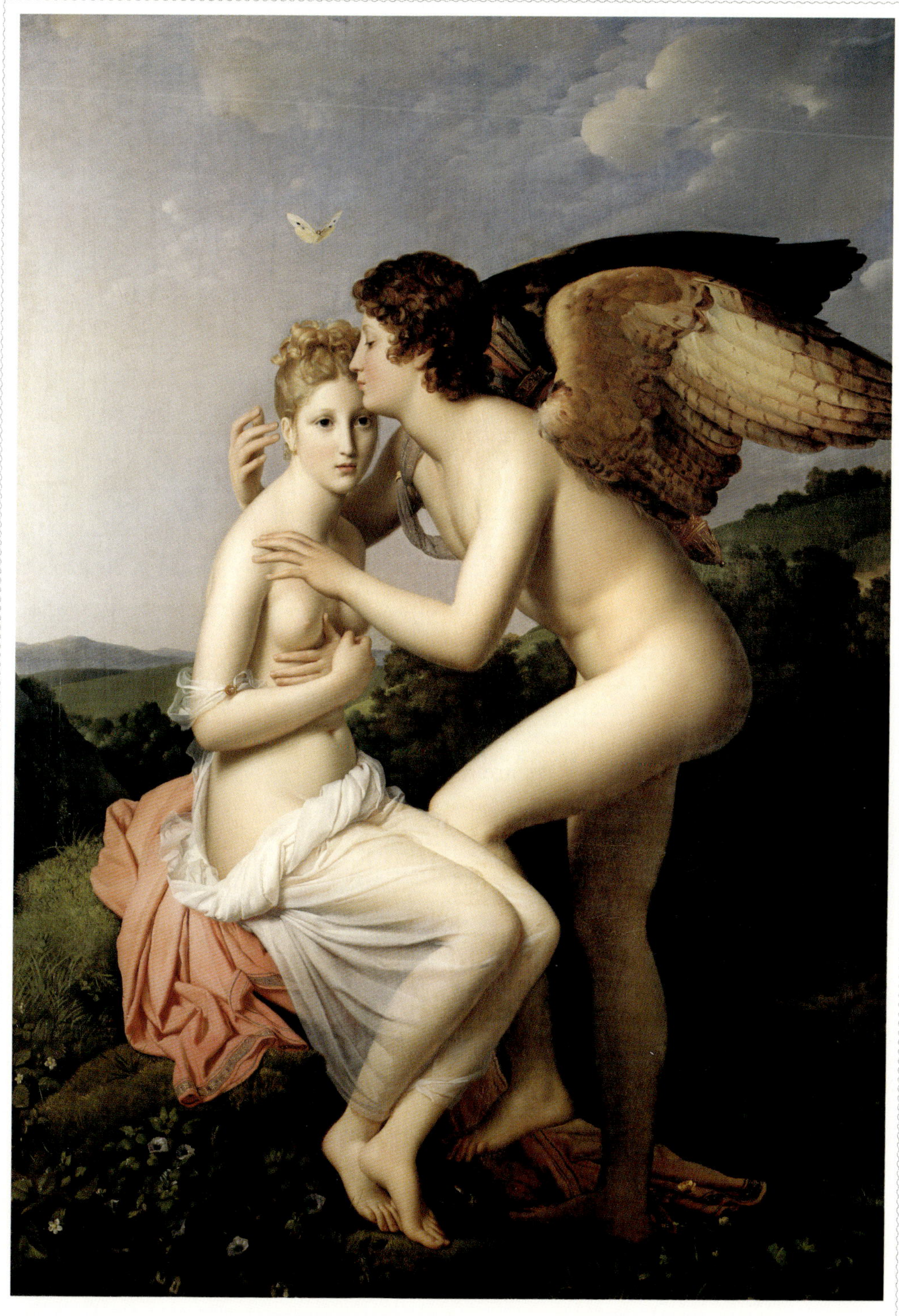

François Gérard CUPID AND PSYCHE, 1798

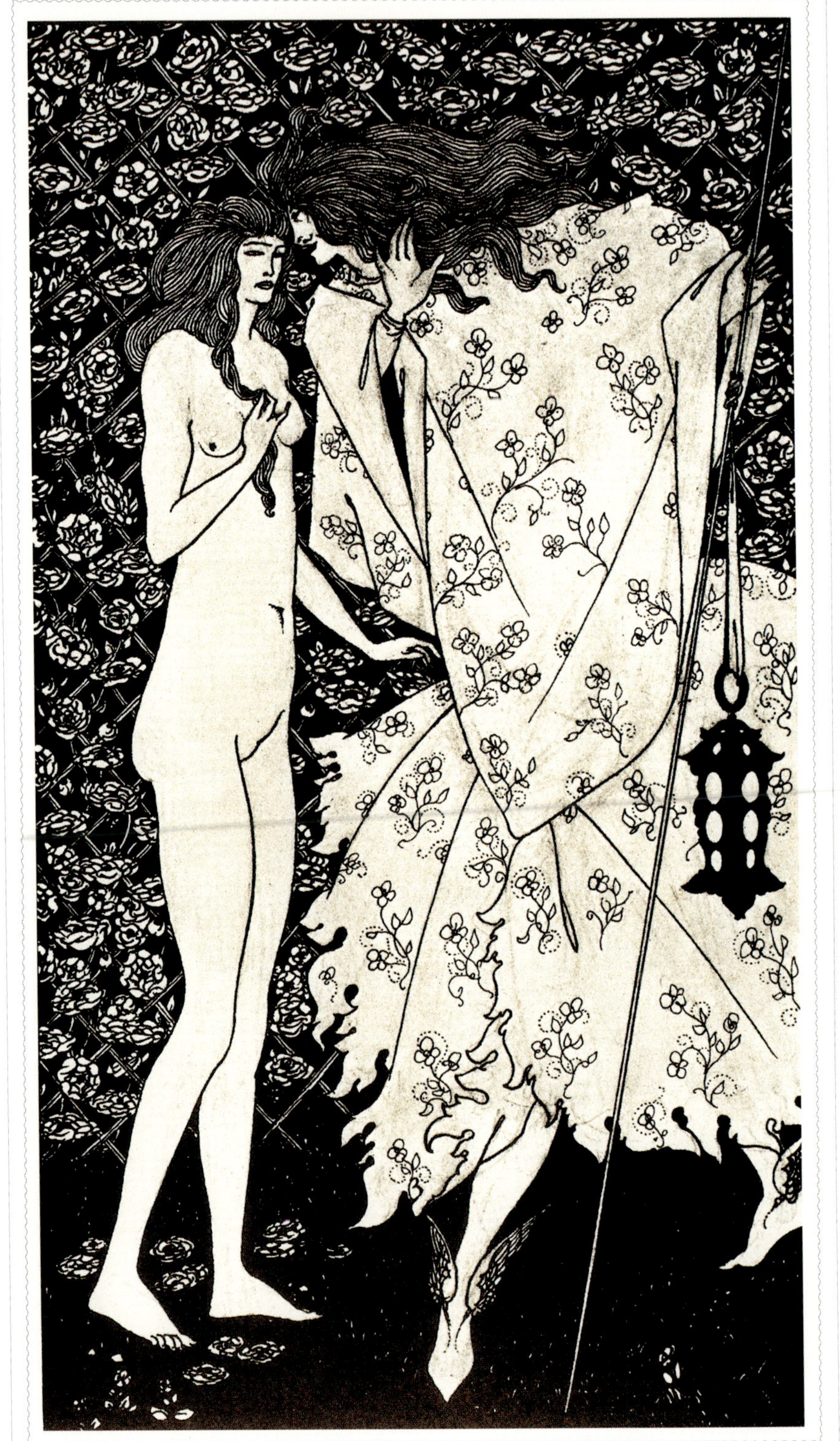

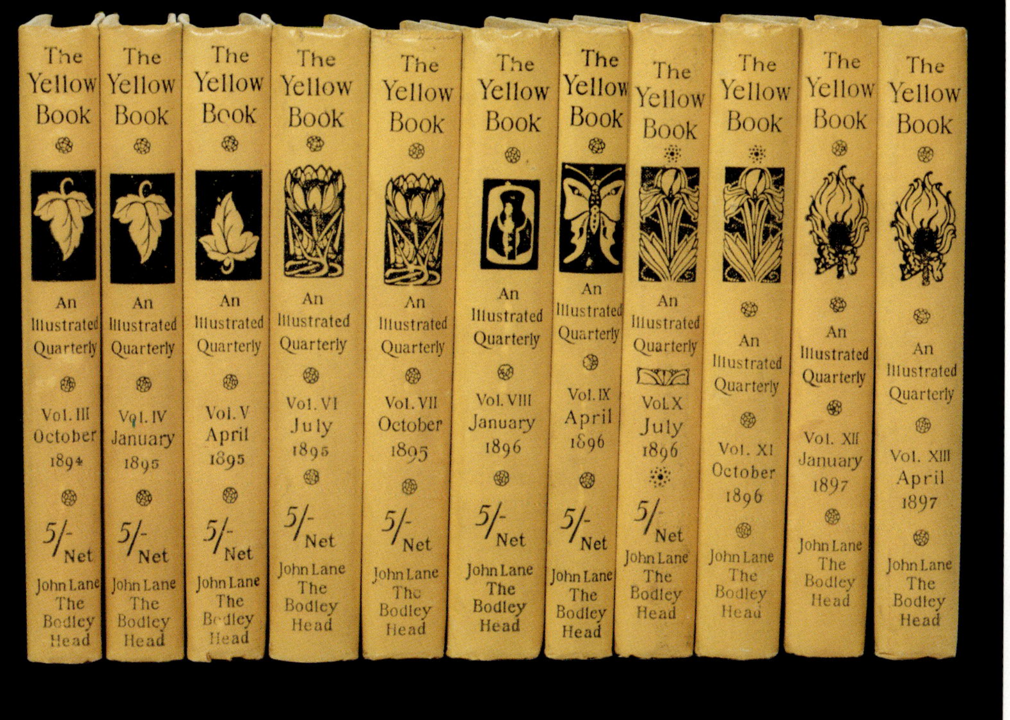

Aubrey Beardsley

OPPOSITE: *THE MYSTERIOUS ROSE GARDEN*, AN ILLUSTRATION FROM *THE YELLOW BOOK*, 1895. ABOVE: SPINE DESIGNS FOR *THE YELLOW BOOK*, VOLUMES II–XIII, PUBLISHED 1894–1897.

When the Wilde trial finally erupted as a national scandal, nobody and nothing ever touched by Oscar's scented glove was safe. While walking from his doorstep to the waiting coach that would deliver him to court, reporters noticed that Wilde held "a yellow book" tucked underneath his arm. This was most likely J. K. Huysmans's classic *A Rebours*, of which the then-current edition sported a bright yellow cover, but unfortunately, in the mounting lynch-mob atmosphere, the difference between the indefinite and the definite article was overlooked. "A yellow book" became *The Yellow Book*, and in the backlash against Wilde, the single most important literary and artistic publication of the 1890s was stamped brutally out of existence.

Beardsley, having illustrated Wilde's *Salomé*, was inextricably connected with the jailed and banished Wilde in the public mind and was assumed to be a homosexual. Ironically, the artist was not merely *not* a close friend or associate of Wilde's, but actively disliked him and would take pains to avoid the portly dandy if he saw him coming. From the viewpoint of the general public, though, this was irrelevant: To have adorned a work by Oscar Wilde was evidently just as bad as having been discovered in flagrante with the poet. Beardsley, horrified by these insinuations, ran into the home of an acquaintance one night, gaunt and haggard and unshaven. Staring through his red-rimmed, haunted eyes into a looking glass, the artist asked of no one in particular if the face he was looking at could be that of a sodomite. Blacklisted by all decent publishers and with *The Yellow Book* now gone, Beardsley was suddenly deprived of both an income and an outlet for his art, while in the midst of emotional turmoil and declining health. *He coughs into his linen handkerchief and stares at the resultant scarlet spatter, poppies standing in the snow.*

It is at this point that the cavalry arrives, too late to save the day but just in time for one last doomed, heroic rally: Leonard Smithers, former lawyer turned smut-publisher, one of the true unsung heroes of pornography. His valiant efforts, following the Wilde trial, to find work for Beardsley, Dowson, and the rest resulted in his publication of a new decadent periodical called *The Savoy*, which

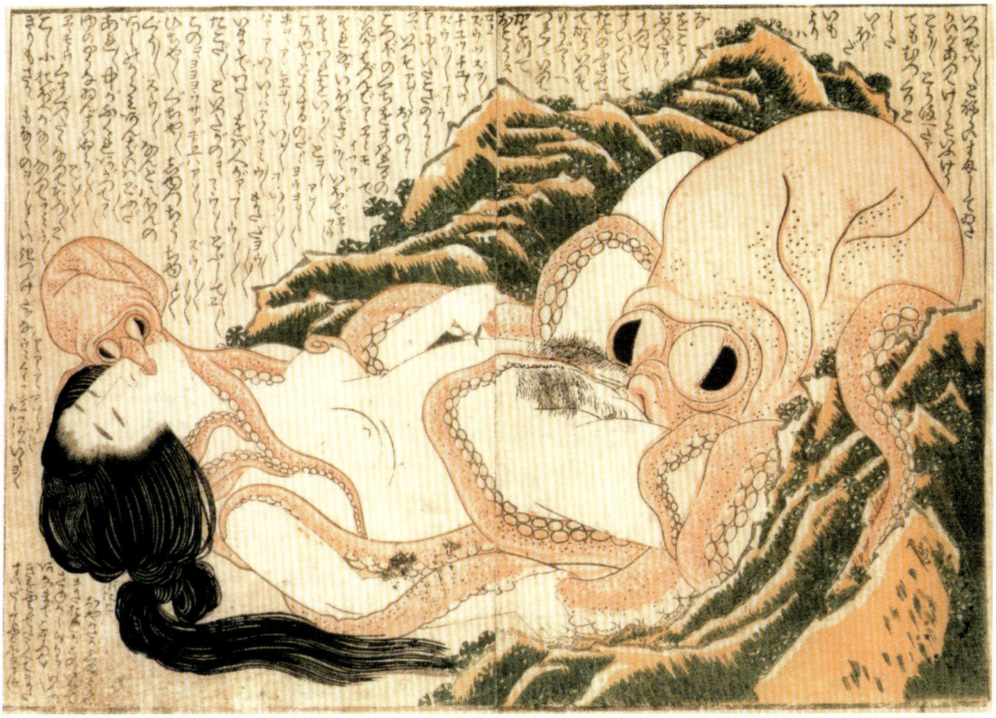

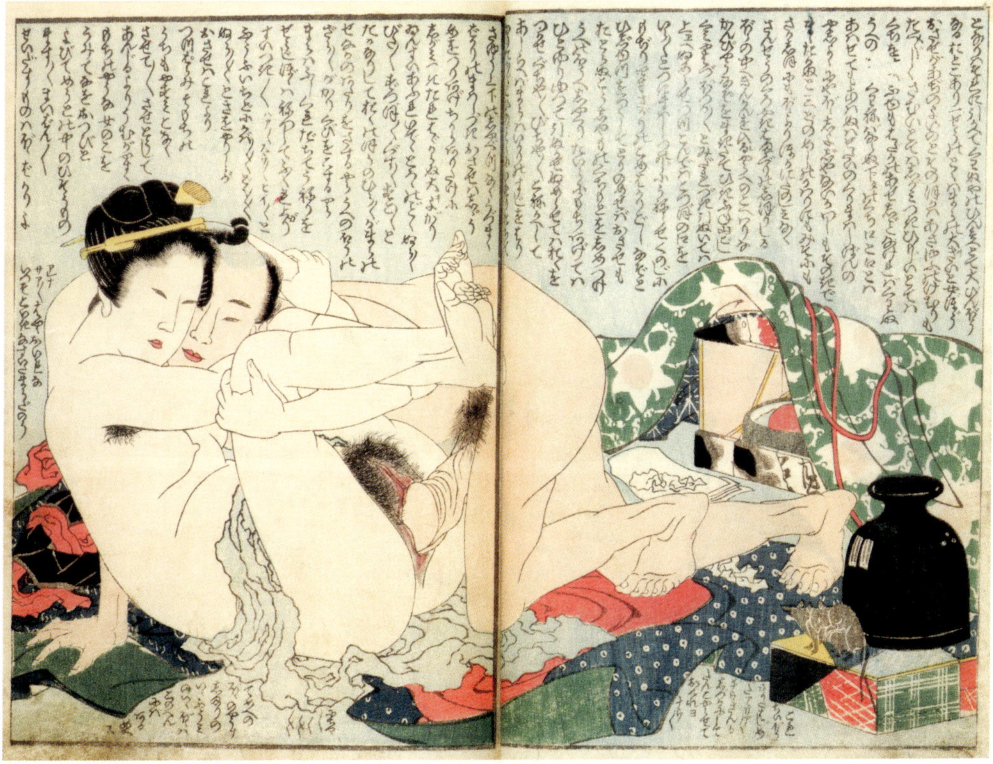

Katsushika Hokusai ABOVE AND OVERLEAF: EROTIC WOODBLOCK PRINTS, 1800

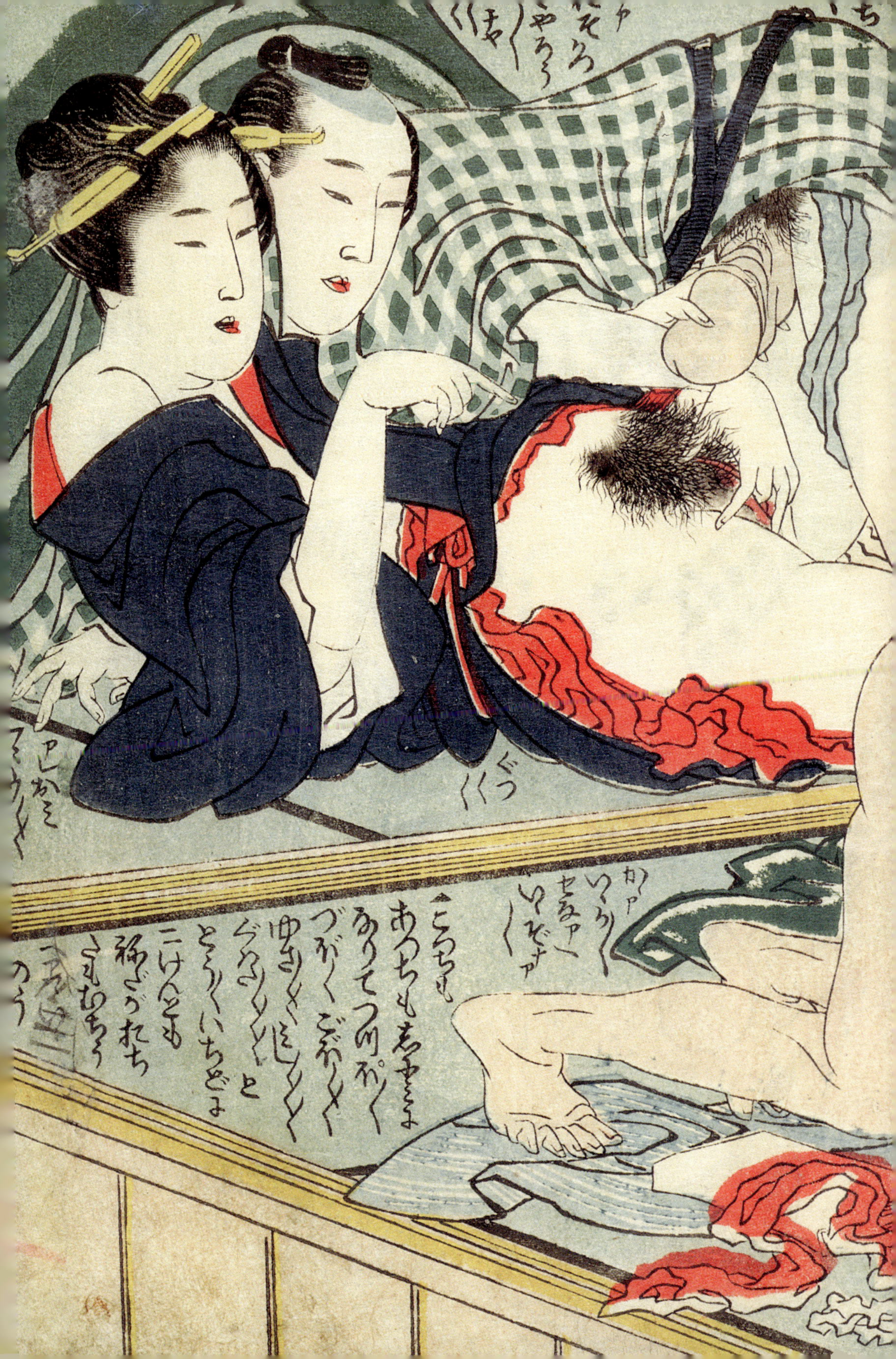

よしやまと〳〵わせ
そうかゝんどう九天之けんの
らだなえをふうかぎ上のみなむくい
一日ひさしのつゞけどりとおりい月じ
ふたりぶ二人ながらいきりあえをふかれ
ばかりで〳〵あらもすけ出してよがりへヱモシ〳〵
なさんせ〳〵そこそのかりみたところのいゝがしでろくの
ところのかう〳〵がそえまゝなそれまづ〳〵アヱアヱア
いゝどうせうアレ〳〵いゝよ〳〵とふとうりれひしと
はぎをついてのさかいろけとおりかふうらんが
ろうぶりと〳〵たまりをひろげくうすぎなそうり
てまわりくよこれめちりアレかく〳〵せなァへ
くびまきさそんさのまらァさとうまうざアレ
一いつびかさのうきァをとおらねうまヱ
くりとろ〳〵ハヱわうろく〳〵
ロまきアモウたくのこつかれ
のけへまうのおさまアせぶん
ヱへろめやさんべヱ屋ヱて〳〵
いく〳〵さん〳〵あきいうそう
てよいふ〳〵どこちくかなげが
ろちがよがりひちやく〳〵ごぶ〳〵
ハウ〳〵〳〵フウ〳〵

succeeded and in many ways surpassed the much-missed *Yellow Book*. For Beardsley, though, while this reprieve from cultural exile was a welcome one, the damage to his confidence and self-esteem had already been done, and this would seem to have had repercussions on the artist's physical well-being, or specifically, his lungs.

In 1898, with Beardsley on his deathbed, his last wishes were that Mabs, his sister Mabel, should take pains to destroy *Lysistrata* and "all obscene works." Subsequent publication of the *Lysistrata* illustrations and of Beardsley's uncompleted pornographic novel (a retelling of the legend of Venus and Tannhäuser that he called *Under the Hill*) suggest that Mabel Beardsley showed considerably more reluctance to purge the erotic from her brother's work than Catherine Blake had shown regarding that of her late husband, and for this we should be grateful to her. Thanks to Mabel, several pieces of exquisite work survive that would not have otherwise. It's still disheartening, however, to consider Aubrey Beardsley going to his grave unnecessarily ashamed of anything in the slim body of sublime and influential work he gave the world. Like Wilde's or Ernest Dowson's, Beardsley's work had only ever enriched human culture with its grace and beauty. Where, in that, was there anything to be ashamed of?

The incoming moral weather, though, dictated otherwise. Around the juncture of the nineteenth and twentieth centuries, the British Empire was at its uneasy peak—the largest empire that the world had ever known, with subsequently massive cultural influence across the globe, for better or, more usually, for worse. Despite the bloated self-important arrogance that seemingly accompanies all empires when they're at the dizzy heights immediately preceding their historically inevitable downfall, Britain was approaching the new century with a whole nest of nagging insecurities: The British Empire was itself falling apart and would be done with by the time that India gained independence in 1947. No one was entirely sure what changes the new century would bring, and no doubt when it came to decadence within the arts, numerous labored parallels with Ancient Rome were drawn. For whatever reason, the new liberalism in the art and writings of the Decadents was seen as symptomatic of a moral blight—an indicator of decline. Thus, with a fierceness born of fear, the Empire struck back through the Wilde trial and its frightened, cowering aftermath, imposing what amounted to a new Puritanism that would have its impact right across the Western world.

In Germany, as an example, the desire to curb and regulate sexual expression took on trappings that, perhaps predictably, were pseudo-scientific. As with K. M. Benkert, who first minted the term 'homosexuality' as an expression to be used by doctors or pathologists, so almost any form of socially unseemly sexuality (which is to say practically all of it) was seen as a disease that might one day be cured by science. An ingenious array of "medical" devices was produced, for instance, to protect the vulnerable youngster from unwelcome incidents of bodily arousal such as those, say, that occur to adolescent boys when they're asleep. While the boy's hands would obviously be strapped securely to the headboard to prevent deliberate acts of masturbation, this did not prevent him from becoming sexually aroused while sleeping, possibly while dreaming, which was clearly a quite unacceptable state of affairs in century's-end Germany. To solve this problem somebody devised a ring with sharp spikes set around the inside surface, which could be placed comfortably around a detumescent penis—but which would impale it if the organ happened to expand for any reason. Very popular with parents of small boys in early twentieth century Germany and Austria, apparently, this form of Sadeian sexual torture during childhood would produce the famously well-balanced generation of young Übermenschen that counted noted sexual deviant Adolf Hitler in its ranks.

Just to recap, then: Sexually progressive cultures gave us mathematics, literature, philosophy, civilization, and the rest, while sexually restrictive cultures gave us the Dark Ages and the Holocaust. Not that I'm trying to load my argument, of course.

While this wave of repression had its victims, it could not prevent the twentieth century from happening nor bringing with it new technologies that would inevitably change all aspects of our lives,

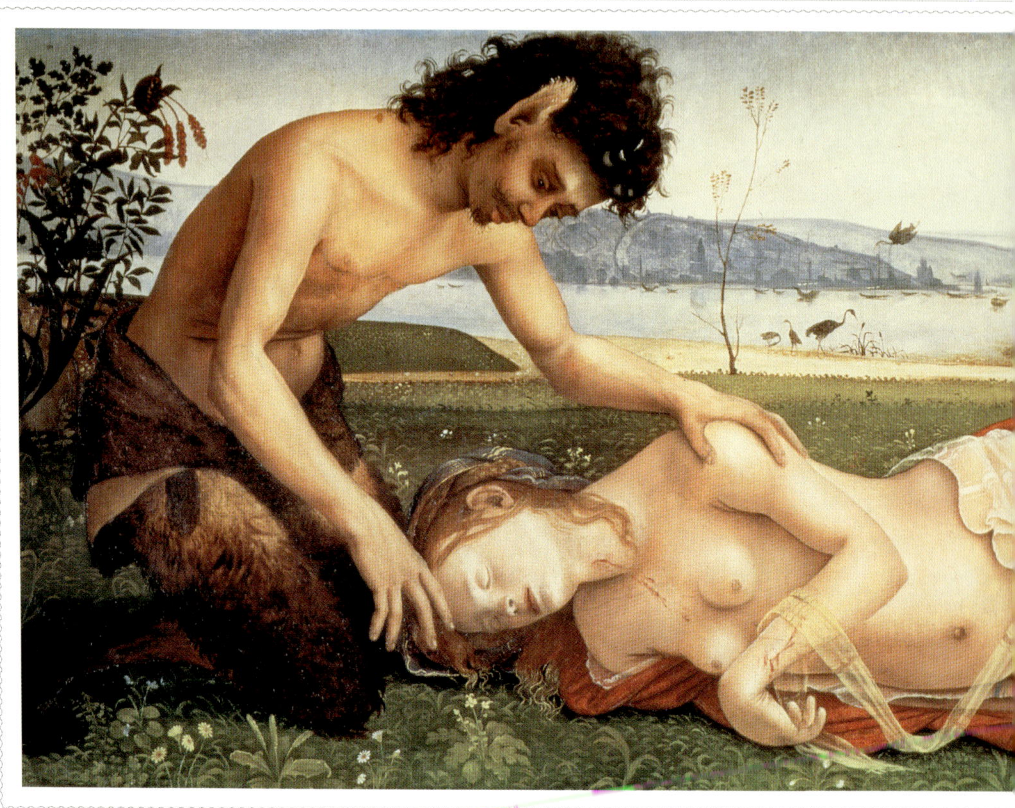

including our pornography. Film had arrived in the late 1800s, giving birth immediately to the first pornographic stag reels, but as with the camera that had come before, the sheer expense of the equipment necessary to produce a halfway-competent blue movie made such efforts a minority affair. It was instead from the developments that had been made in William Caxton's print technology that the next surge of sexually explicit life would come. Newer and cheaper modes of printing, such as the mimeograph, were coming into play, which meant that publishing would soon become a much more democratic process and was no longer solely the province of the wealthy and the cultured.

In the 1930s came the boom in what was known as "mushroom" publishing in Britain, an equivalent to the much larger pulp explosion

Piero di Cosimo *A SATYR MOURNING OVER A NYMPH*, CIRCA 1495

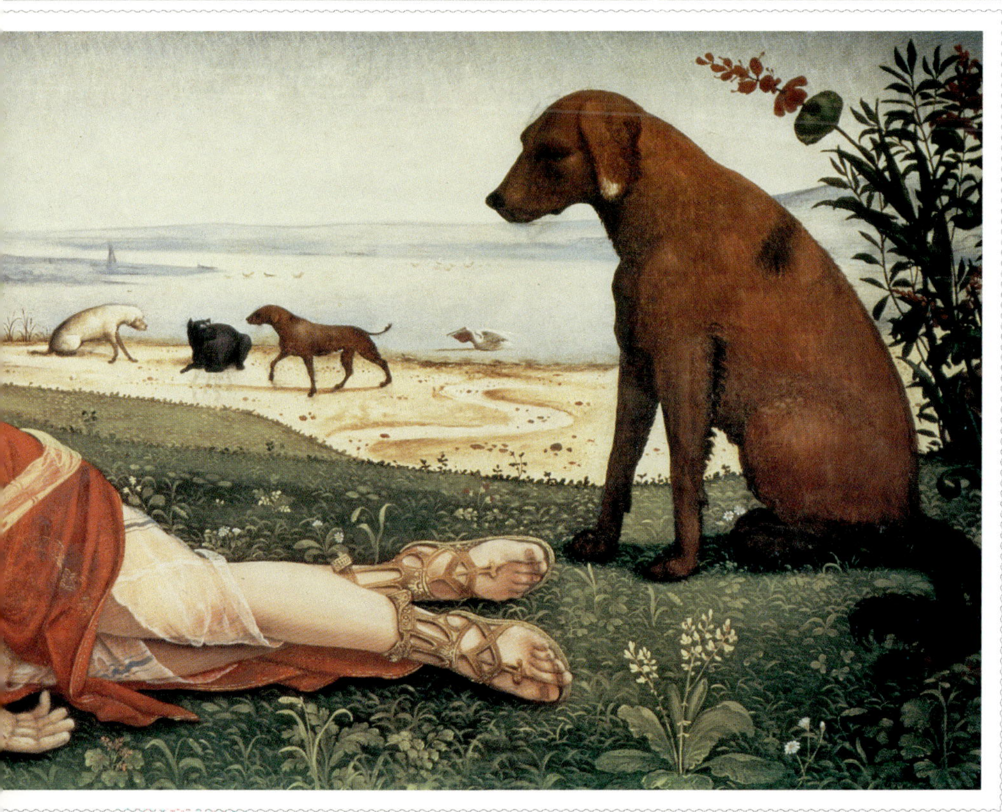

that was happening in the United States. Although both countries had their rudimentary laws on obscenity in place by this time, in both cases the laws were so ill-defined as to allow a great deal of room for interpretation. Raciness was tolerated up to soft-core levels, although in such foggily delineated territory it was easy to cross over lines unwittingly and find yourself the focus of a moral panic, such as happened with the "spicy" pulps that came out in the United States, or with the Hank Janssen novels. The public's thirst for pornographic fare was evidently undiminished, but by brute overreaction and a zero-tolerance policy (such as the prosecution that saw British saucy seaside postcard veteran Donald McGill convicted for his smutty innuendoes), the authorities could just about hold down the tin lid on their quaking, seething pressure-cooker.

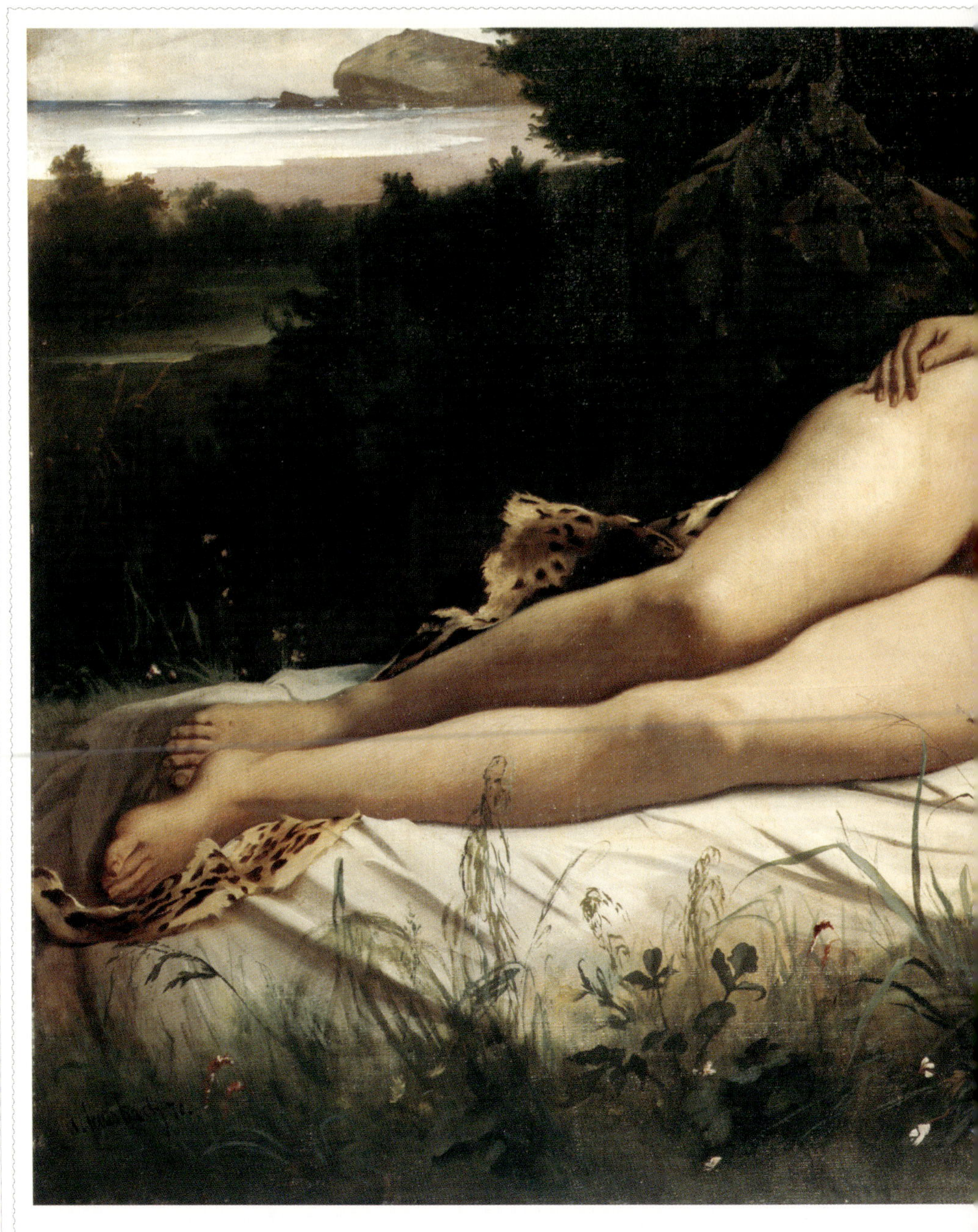

Anselm Feuerbach RECUMBENT NYMPH, 1870

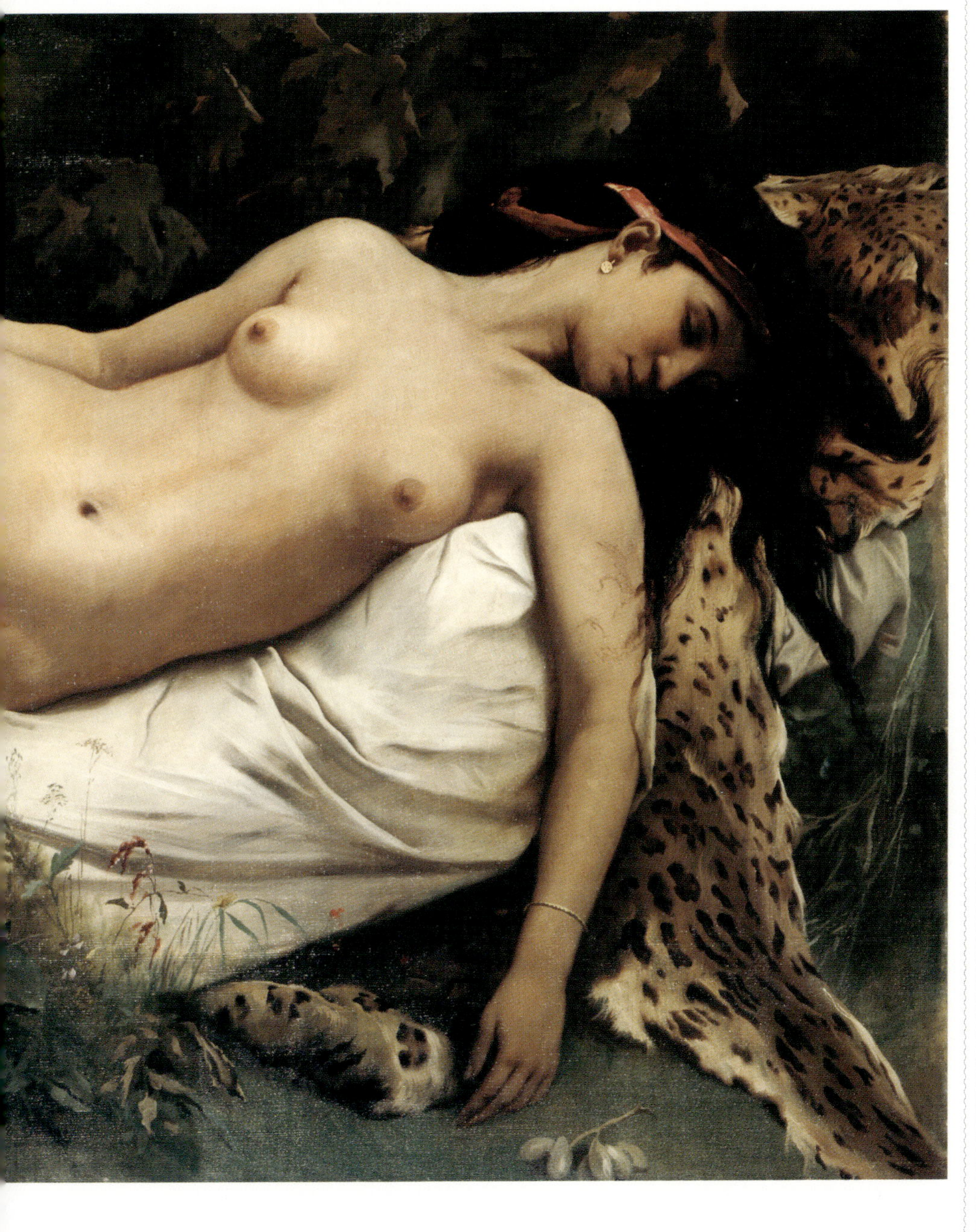

This is not to say there weren't steamy escapes from time to time. The subterranean world of hardcore pornographic publishing had weathered all the ups and downs of the new century, remaining more or less untouched by virtue of its near-invisibility. Other than a smattering of reprints from the previous century and intermittent bursts of low-grade new material, however, there's not much to recommend the porno output of the 1930s save for the phenomenon of eight-page pamphlets churned out in America during this period and known as "Tijuana Bibles," possibly because it was assumed that sex and anything associated with it started out in Tijuana, Mexico.

The eight-pagers, crude material crudely produced, are nonetheless a fascinating way-stage in the evolution of both comics and erotica. Though various apocryphal accounts exist of how these books came into being, the most winning and endearing version is the one in which three ladies clandestinely form a partnership to supplement their incomes, with one woman handling the writing, one the drawing, and the third one handling the business/distribution end of the arrangement. Whether this is true or not, the fact remains that in the Tijuana Bibles we can see a socially mischievous spark that would in time provide the basis for a whole American tradition of first-rate inflammatory satire told in comic form.

The best-remembered of the Tijuana Bibles were the ones that featured well-known characters from daily comic strips, shakily rendered in what were still fair approximations of the styles used by the artists who had worked on the originals. The great appeal of showing thoroughly non-sexual figures such as Blondie, Jiggs, or Popeye taking part in pornographic skits lies in the greater contrast, with the sexual content seeming dirtier when in the context of some previously spotless cultural icon. There is also the subversive pleasure that is to be had in puncturing the anodyne and sexless vision of society presented by the Sunday funnies, and it seems entirely likely that when Harvey Kurtzman drafted up the blueprint for his seminal *MAD* comic in the 1950s, the eight-pagers were an influential part of the satiric mix. Kurtzman's attack

Lucas Cranach the Elder *VENUS AND CUPID*, CIRCA 1537

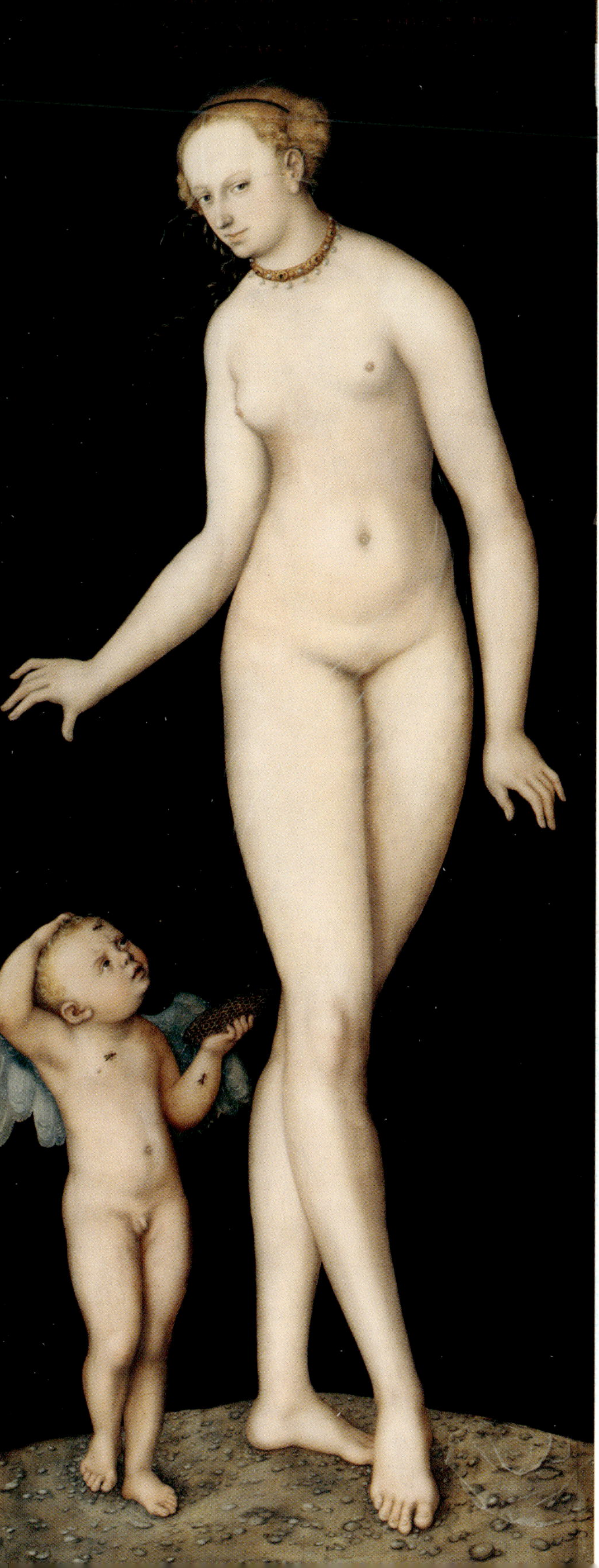

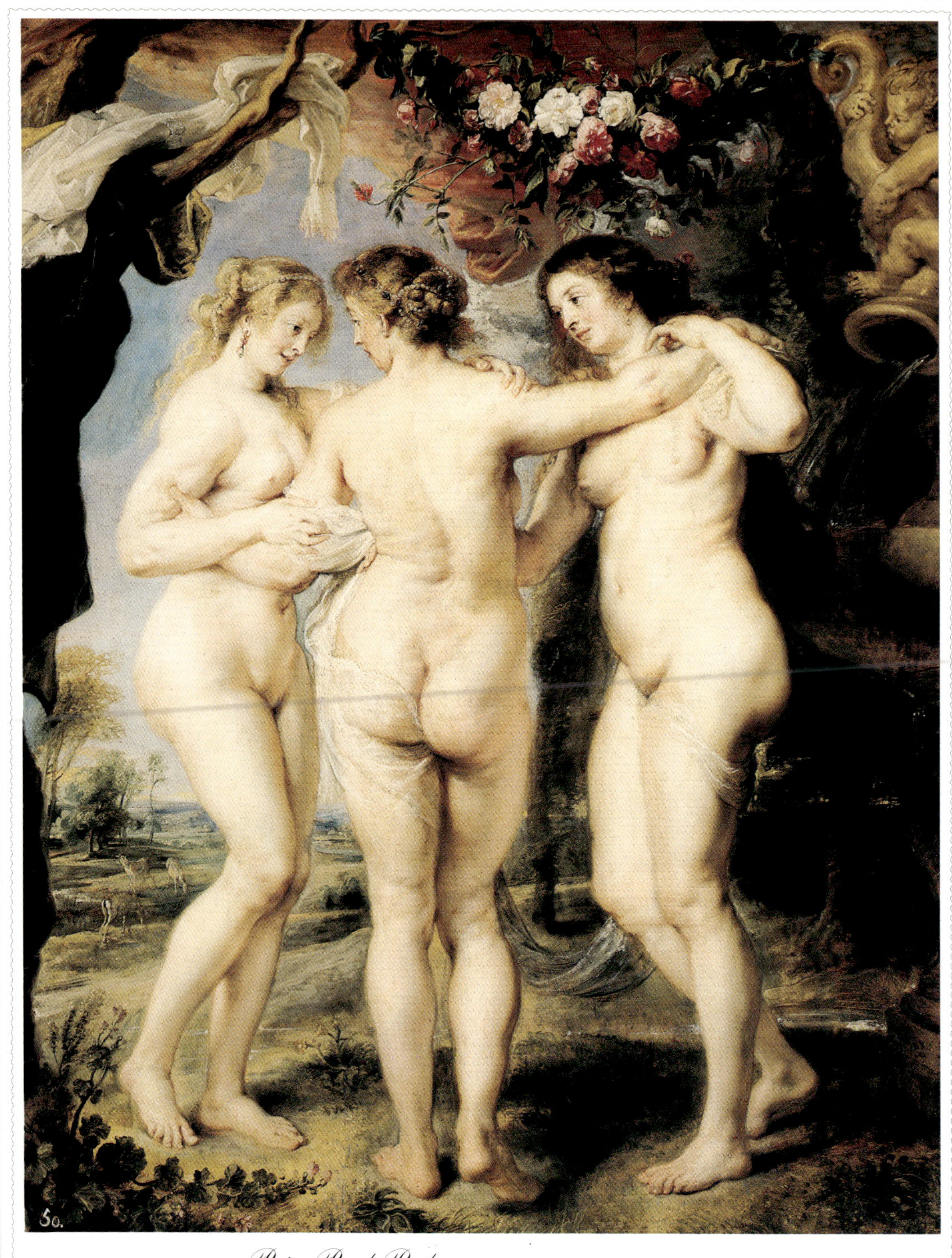

Peter Paul Rubens *THE THREE GRACES*, 1636–38

on Archie (which reputedly ensured punitive treatment of the E. C. Comics line by a draconian comics code authority presided over by the Archie Comics publishers) presented the allegedly "typical teenager" as a high school protection racketeer, with Betty and Veronica as reefer-smoking jailbait; it was a portrayal that could quite easily have stepped out of an eight-pager, albeit an eight-pager where the flow of sexuality was now only an undercurrent and where the immensely talented Bill Elder did a far superior job of reproducing and subverting the whole Archie style than had the gifted Tijuana amateurs preceding him.

Besides a cast of characters culled from newspaper comic strips, the Tijuana Bible pamphlets also utilized contemporary actresses and actors such as Mae West and Laurel & Hardy as their featured players. Interestingly, the 1930s criminal celebrity such as Baby-Face Nelson or John Dillinger had his own subgenre, playing to the public's obvious affection for a glamorous crook and also to the aura of near-mythic sexual potency with which such figures were surrounded in the popular imagination. In this combination of a wildly antisocial hero figure with the visceral rush of unbridled pornography, the Tijuana Bibles prefigured the comics underground that would erupt, in San Francisco, in another thirty years or so.

Back in the early to middle twentieth century, however, the erotic urges in society were finding their most lively manners of expression in burlesque theater and, a little later, in the "nudie-cutie" movies that burlesque had played its part in giving birth to. Through the 1950s and the 1960s, maverick directors such as Russ Meyer almost managed to provide a voice for the unconscious dream-life of America, its libidinous impulses stirred into a demented slapstick of violence and sex that was at once exuberant and infantile, marked by a kind of innocence, at least compared with all the joyless, dead-eyed fare served up for us today. Justly described as a "rural Fellini," Meyer seems to have had a specific private goddess-image that was given generous flesh in his iconic women like Tura Satana or Kitten Natividad. Just as with Robert Crumb a decade later, Meyer's enshrining of one female body type appears to hark back to the primal origins of the erotic, to Bog Venus with a shiny leather makeover and captured not in stone but in celluloid.

In 1950s culture, powerful sexual undertones were evident, sprung up in opposition to the stifling and sexless Eisenhower/McMillan ethos of the times. Writers such as Hubert Selby, Jr., and Henry Miller, who'd produced work in the 1930s and the 1940s that was banned on publication, were beginning to find an appreciative new audience and sometimes even foreign publishers, such as the Olympia Press, founded by Maurice Girodias. Hugh Hefner's *Playboy* was attempting to establish soft-core porn as an upmarket lifestyle statement, and a new wave of "sick" comedy was coming into being that would find its apogee in the uncensored and occasionally brilliant rants of Lenny Bruce. Meanwhile, in Harvey Kurtzman's *MAD* there was a sharp new synthesis of hip and Jewish humor that took sexual references as a standard part of its comedic repertoire, as in the Kurtzman parody of Julius Caesar in which a centurion crying "Someone's comingeth!" is answered by

a word balloon from somewhere out of panel reading "Ooh, I'm dyingeth!" Elsewhere, new and exciting music spilled out of the radios—black-influenced and sexual with its label, "rock 'n' roll," simply another euphemism for the sexual act, as "jazz" itself had been. And most importantly of all, in San Francisco in 1955, the poet Lawrence Ferlinghetti started publishing as City Lights Books in North Beach, the city's famously bohemian Italian quarter that had previously been inhabited by anti-Mussolini anarchists.

Having heard the young New York poet Allen Ginsberg's first public performance of his William Blake–inspired work *Howl* at the Six Gallery in 1955, the impressed Ferlinghetti published it through City Lights Books in November 1956. Despite the minimal attention that the book at first received—hardly surprising for a first work by an unknown author in the pretty much neglected field of poetry—by June 1957 a police raid carried out on City Lights Books and a subsequent trial for obscenity pushed *Howl and Other Poems* to the forefront of the nation's consciousness. Judge Clayton Horn, surprisingly, ruled that a work could not be deemed obscene if it possessed "the slightest redeeming social significance."

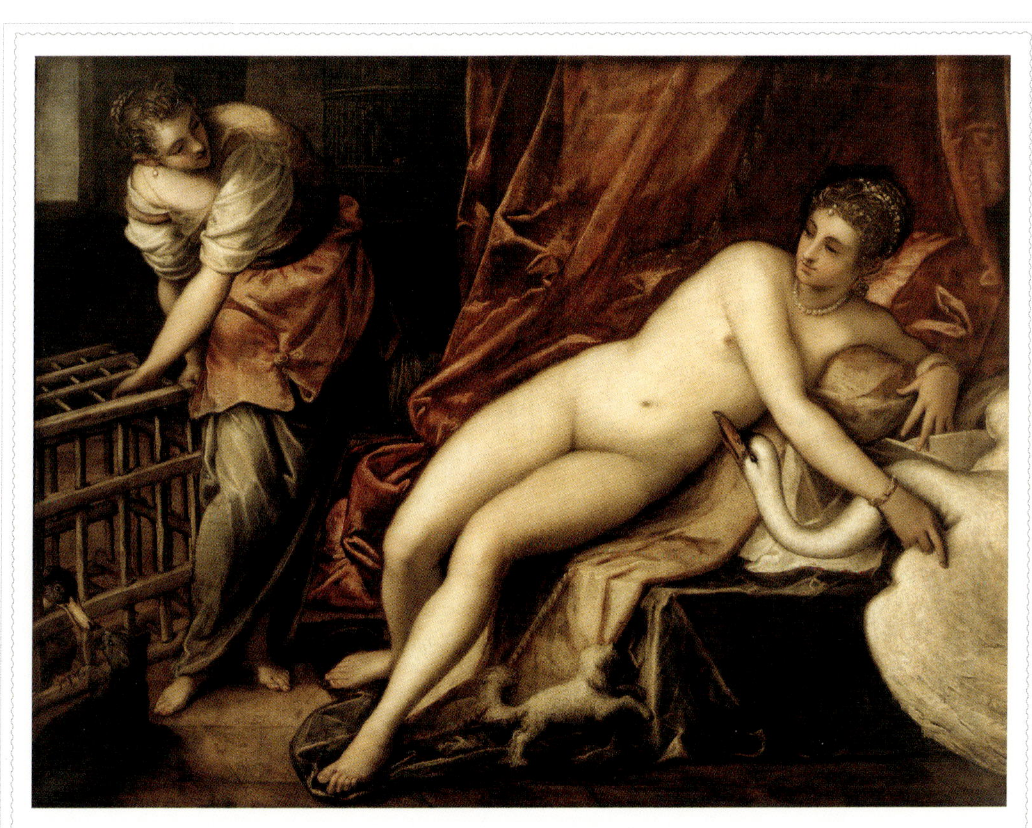

Jacopo Rubusti Tintoretto *LEDA AND THE SWAN*, CIRCA 1570

Judge Horn's decision meant that City Lights could put out *Howl* and many other controversial pieces without fear of damaging reprisals from those in authority. Although some writings were still too extreme to publish for a year or two, such as the first ten chapters of *The Naked Lunch* by William S. Burroughs, which had been turned down by the Chicago Literary Revue, the ruling meant that the Beat writers could now crystallize around Ferlinghetti's premises at 261 Columbus Avenue and spark what is possibly the most exciting literary movement of the twentieth century. It also meant that an important legal precedent had been established, granting sexual material immunity from prosecution if it could be shown as socially significant or of artistic merit.

This was the defense successfully adopted some years later in the widely celebrated English court case over D. H. Lawrence's *Lady Chatterley's Lover*, during which the prosecuting counsel summarized a still-prevailing attitude toward pornography when he suggested that no decent person would allow their "wives or servants" to read such a work. This one remark, betraying as it did a ludicrously antiquated and Victorian view of social matters, almost certainly convinced the jury to vote on the side of the defense. The point of view behind the prosecution's statement is that while "we," being white males of a certain age and social standing, are far too evolved to be depraved by such material, its probable effects upon those morally more feeble than ourselves (such as the young, the working classes, foreigners, or women) would be ruinous.

While as a work of modern beatnik poetry *Howl* could be safely overlooked by the majority of average citizens, the *Lady Chatterley* trial meant that most homes in the Western world would come to own a much-thumbed copy of what is in fact a relatively minor work by D. H. Lawrence. Sexual subject matter, in the public's eye, had become normalized, which would open the floodgates to the rush of sexually suggestive or explicit television programs, movies, books, and pop-song lyrics that would help define the 1960s, although obviously such progress did not go entirely unopposed. Books were still banned, films were still censored, and at one of London's practically unheard-of exhibitions of erotic art

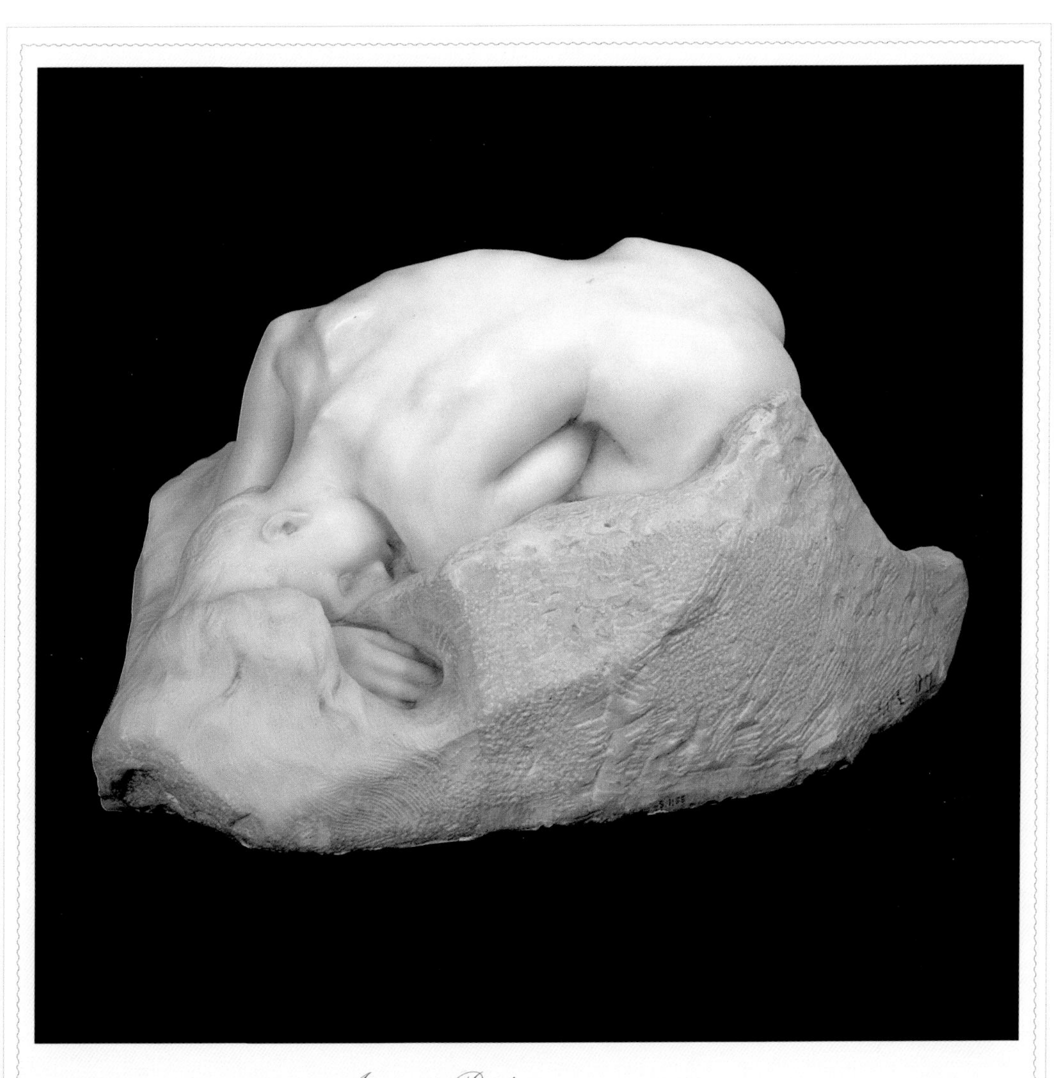

Auguste Rodin LA DANAÏDE, 1885

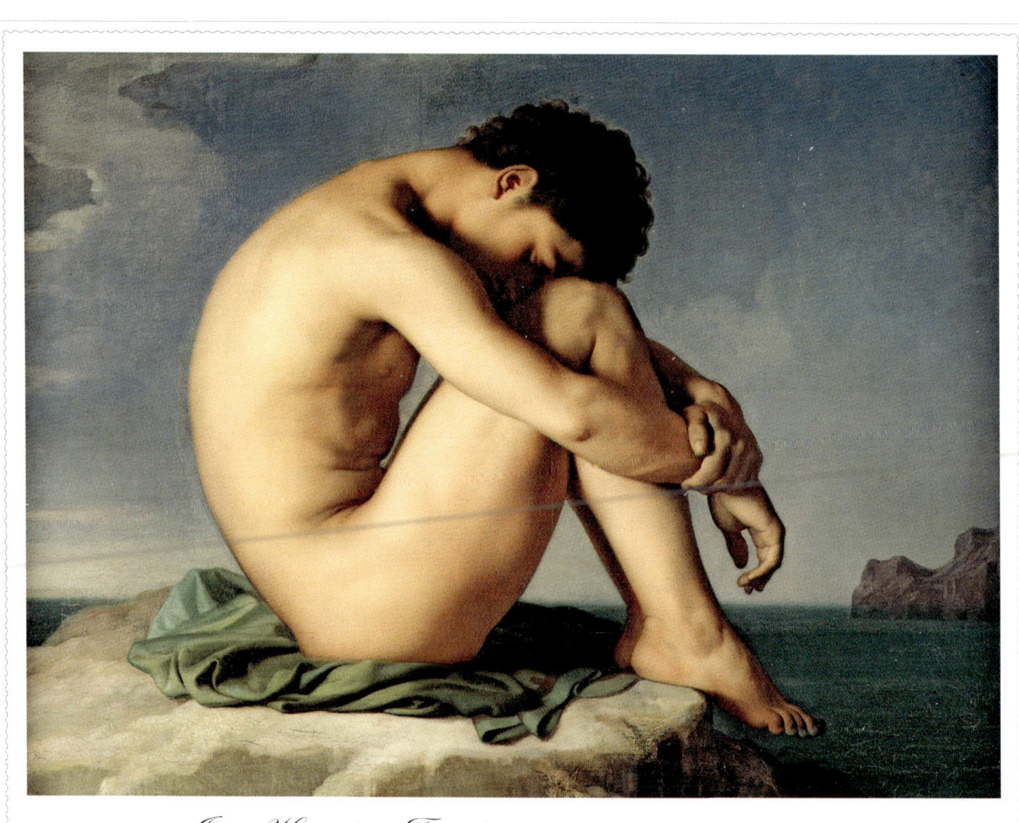

Jean-Hippolyte Flandrin YOUNG MAN SITTING BY THE SEA, 1836

during the sixties, doodles by John Lennon were seized by police, along with several *Lysistrata* prints by poor old Aubrey Beardsley, who had been dead seventy years by then. Organizations such as the National Viewers and Listeners Association headed by self-publicizing, self-appointed moral guardian Mary Whitehouse would put pressure on the BBC to tone down certain television shows or to remove Scott Walker's version of the Jacques Brel classic *Jackie* from the radio playlists lest its references to "authentic queers and phoney virgins" should corrupt the young.

The running battle faced by sexual expression during the "permissive sixties" is an indication of how deeply feelings ran upon the issue. Evidently, the same social squeamishness regarding sex that the Marquis de Sade had made his target back in revolutionary France was still a soft spot that those wishing to critique society could do far worse than to attack. The hippie movement, welling up in the mid-sixties around various reference points, including Aubrey Beardsley's art nouveau extravagances, William Blake, and Allen Ginsberg's howled response to Blake, was quick to seize on sexual rebellion as a favorite mode of confrontation.

This is not to imply that a font of functional hippie-porn did not spring up. It did, although its manifestations were often subterranean to a degree that caused nary a ripple on the surface of public consciousness. *Fuck You: A Magazine of the Arts* represented Ed Sander's "total assault on culture," something he would later take musical with the Fugs, whose calls for group gropes of every description were greeted with jubilance. Leonore Kandel's *Love Book*, a slim volume of erotic poetry, inexplicably prosecuted in San Francisco, seemed almost the last gasp of the new puritans, although they continued to issue intermittent squeaks (before re-emerging with a roar). By the time Essex House began to issue true hippie porn—David Meltzer's Agency trilogy, Charles Bukowski's *Notes of a Dirty Old Man*, Philip José Farmer's *Image of the Beast*—the entire concept of porn-as-writing seemed to be a dead letter. This was largely due to the efforts of Barney Rossett and Grove Press at redefining the boundaries of acceptable literature. Grove Press went to trial on *Chatterley*, *Tropic of Cancer*, and *Naked Lunch*,

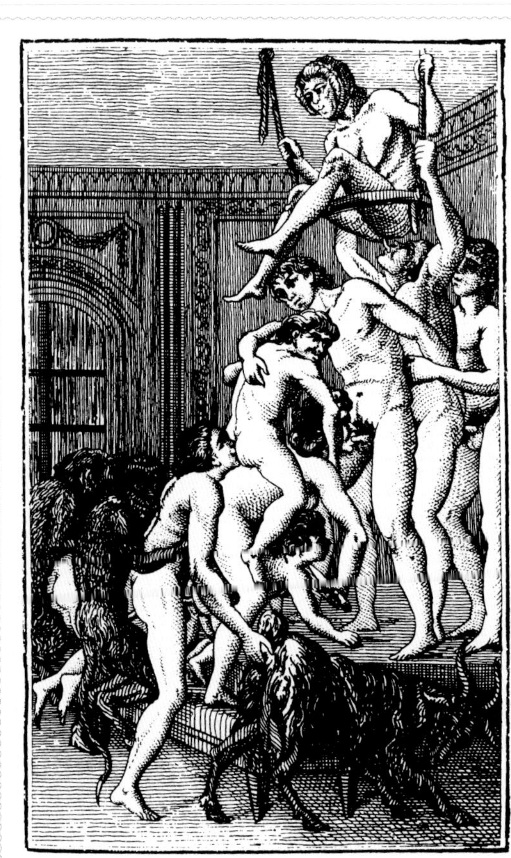

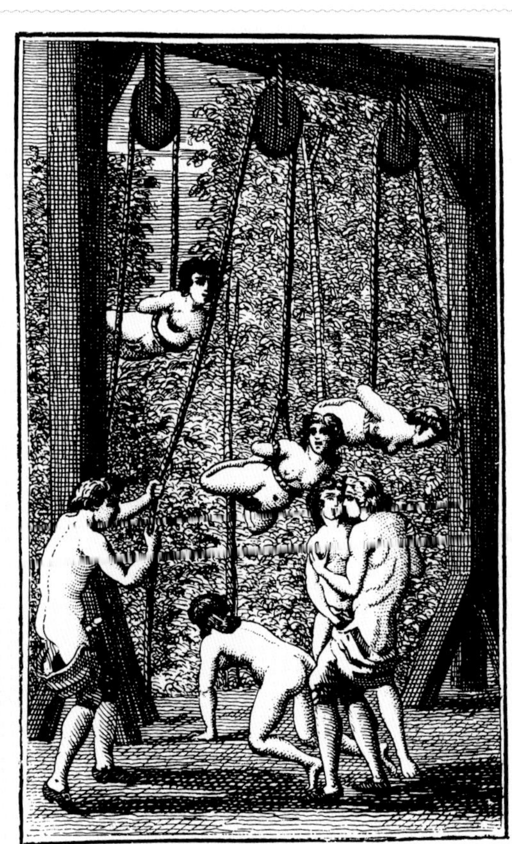

Marquis (Donatien Alphonse François) de Sade

ABOVE AND OPPOSITE: ETCHINGS FROM *JULIETTE*, 1800

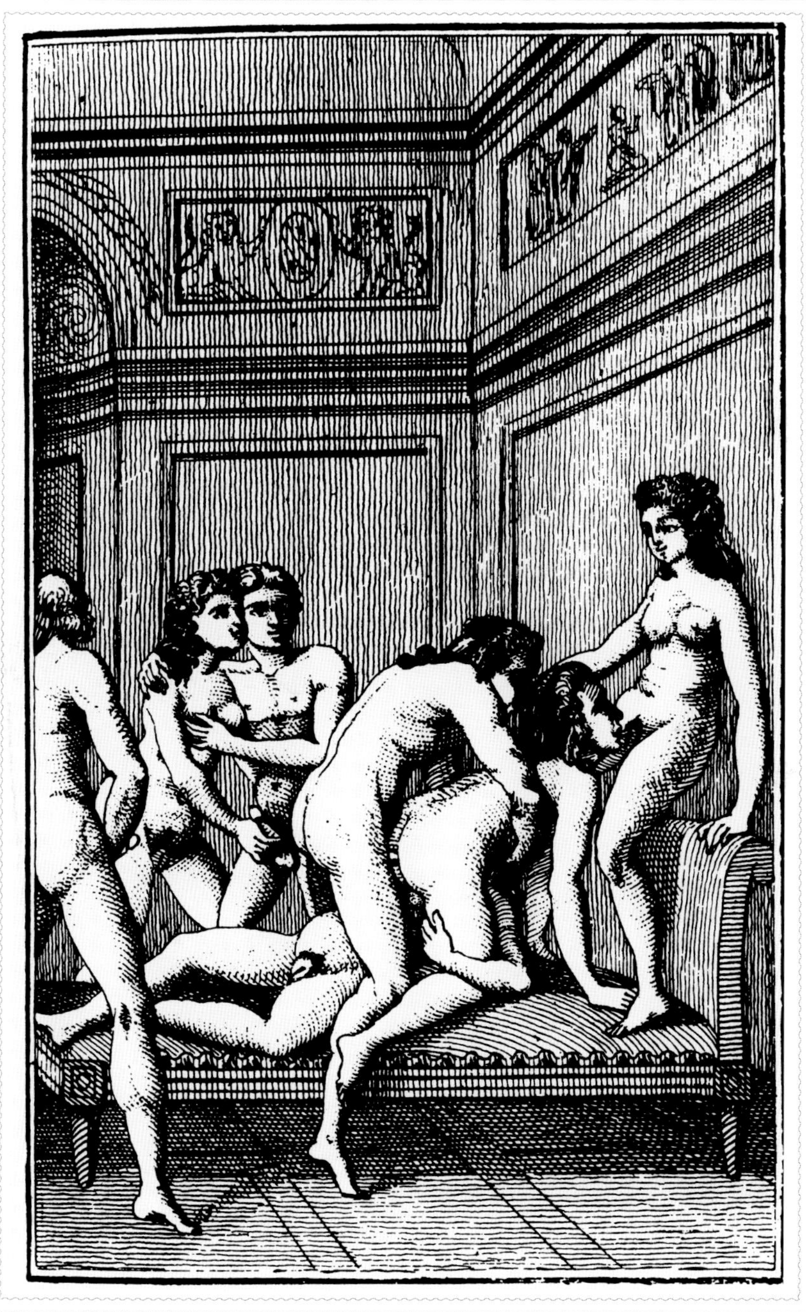

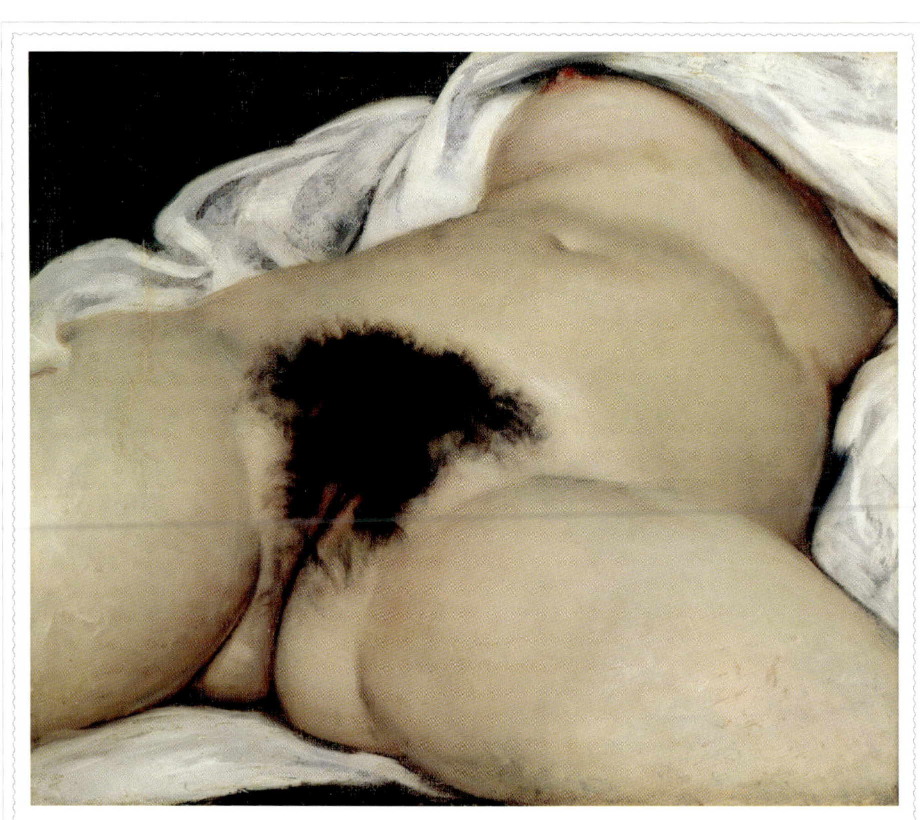

Gustave Courbet THE ORIGIN OF THE WORLD, 1866

winning each case and pushing the frontiers a little further each time. But, indeed, a picture is worth a thousand words.

Nowhere is this counter-cultural assault on sexual conformity better exemplified than in the early comic strips of the extraordinary Robert Crumb, whose pioneering efforts in the underground press turned out work that would prove seminal in every sense. Using a reassuringly familiar and therefore highly subversive style, Crumb gleefully submerged himself in the most flagged-off and restricted waters of the mass unconscious, serving up a vision of America as seen through sexually obsessive eyes, peopled by Snoids and nubile Yetis, with its most forbidden Joe Blow urges dragged out from behind suburbia's concealing drapes, set down in black and white for everyone to see. That Crumb's work was received enthusiastically across the social spectrum would suggest that after the initial shock had worn off, many people found it was a vision that they recognized. They knew, in the contemporary phrase, where Crumb was coming from.

While there were obvious precursors for the underground cartoon explosion in *MAD* comics, Tijuana Bibles, and the fanzine press that Crumb had been a part of, it was Crumb who set the bar for the cartoonists who would follow him, with the release of *Zap* #*1*, peddled from a baby carriage by the artist up and down the freak-encrusted length of Haight Street. Just as with the Sex Pistols almost a decade later, Crumb's work was the catalyst that launched the equally extreme careers of those who followed him. Crumb's work in *Zap*, along with that of gifted cronies such as S. Clay Wilson, Spain, or Robert Williams, plus the many undergrounds that *Zap* inspired, would turn out to be a high-tide line in pornography, created cheerfully with an intent that was both social and artistic. (The brilliant underground cartoonist Sharon Rudahl, using the nom de plume Mary Sativa, wrote *The Acid Temple Ball*, a remarkable novel—published as part of the Olympia Press's "Traveller's Companion" series—that lovingly recounted a woman's sexual experiences while under different combinations of illicit substances.) When the comics undergrounds at last gave up the ghost in the late 1970s, there would be nothing of real energy or spirit that would rise to take their place. Crumb soldiered valiantly on in *Weirdo* and in other publications, but although his work remained as marvelous as ever (and, in fact, continued to improve and to progress), there was the sense now of a solitary maestro laboring in isolation, rather than that of a figurehead with a whole socio-artistic movement surging up behind him.

By and large, what happened in the 1970s was that the hard-won sexual freedoms of the previous decades, fought for on grounds of ideology, became—predictably—a booming market ripe for exploitation. Obviously encouraged by the growth of sexual expression in the arts during the sixties, moviemakers in the seventies decided that the lowly porn film could be wrapped in bigger budgets and improved production values. It could be re-branded, dressed up in a way that would suggest artistic merit, and by this means could become for the first time mass-market cinema. In offerings such as *The Devil in Miss Jones, The Opening of Misty Beethoven, Behind the Green Door,* and a scattering of others, porn directors tried with varying degrees of success to transcend the trashy, dopey limitations of their chosen genre. Smoother camera work and more imaginative sets combined with vestiges of genuine acting talent and at least some semblance of a screenplay to create works that appeared artistic, although only when compared with all the drooling half-witted porn films that had come before.

Even so, the public seemed to like the new availability of porno in the mainstream and responded with enough enthusiasm to allow such movies to proliferate—right up until the point where the real age of Traci Lords came out. Defenses of artistic or social significance were useless when confronted by an actual statutory offense, and with this chink in porno's arty armor opened up by the authorities, the industry seems to have beaten an immediate retreat, with the big-budget porn flick rapidly consigned to history.

Of course, by then the 1980s were just around the corner, and the porno movie would be rescued by the massive rise of the home video market, but its emphasis and its agenda would be changed accordingly. Whereas the improved production values of the 1970s

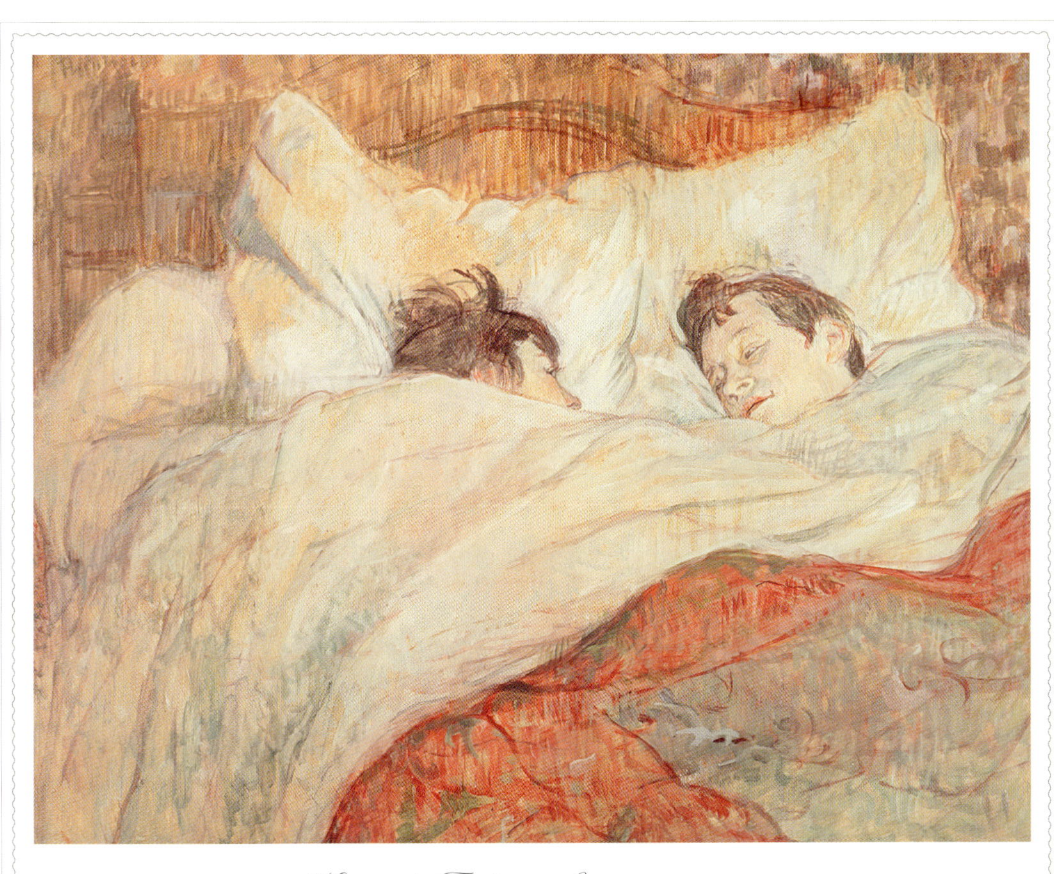

Henri de Toulouse-Lautrec THE BED, 1893

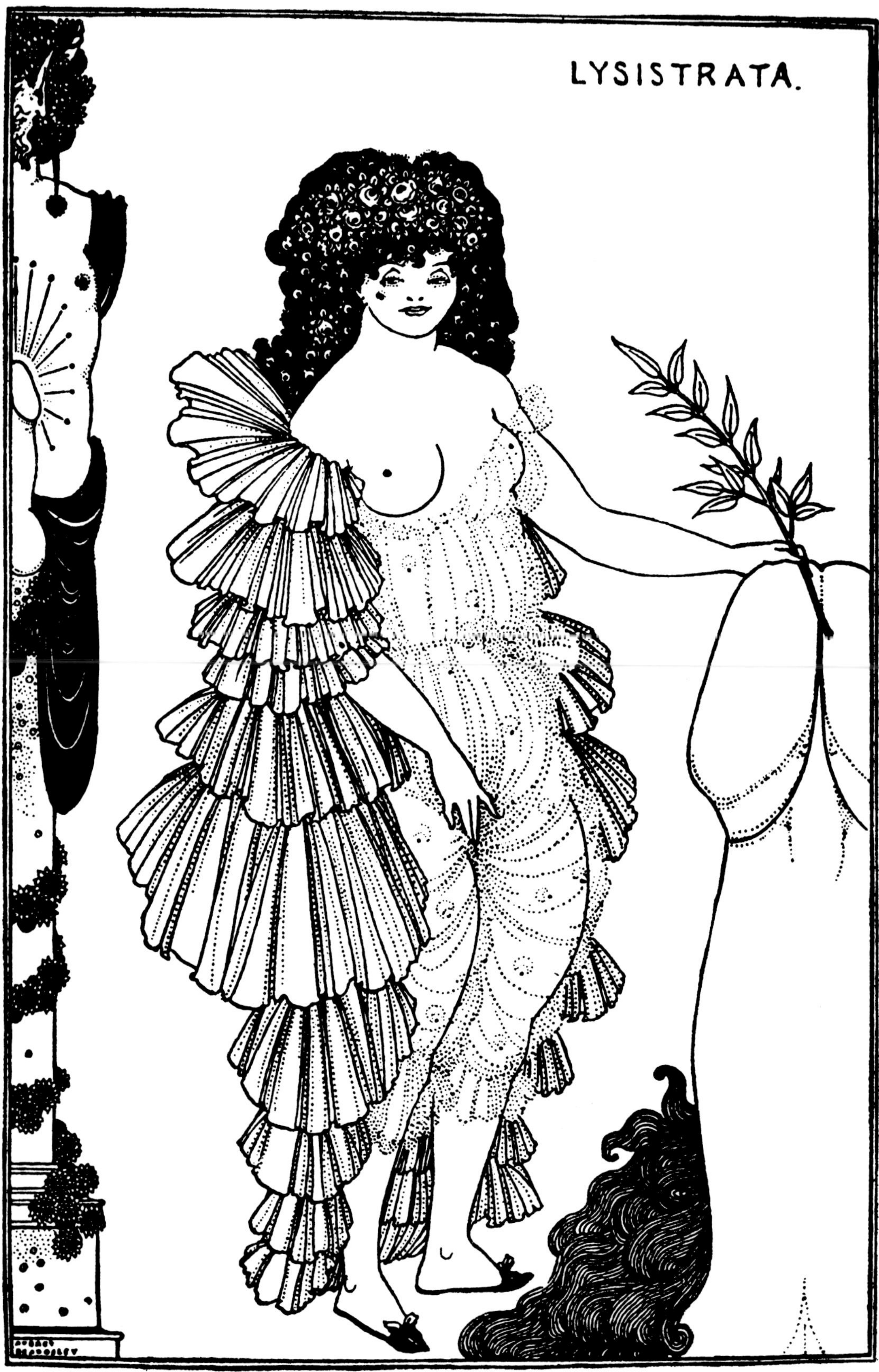
LYSISTRATA.

had been designed to draw in a crossover mainstream audience to the cinemas, home video viewers were identified, perhaps in part correctly, as a captive and addicted market that was entirely undiscriminating in its viewing habits. Subtly yet importantly, the audience's view of itself also changed. While sitting in a crowded cinema watching pornography amongst a hundred other normal individuals or couples could conceivably be quite a liberating communal experience and an indicator of one's liberal tolerance and sophistication, watching a porn movie all alone behind closed shutters is a very different matter, and it invokes a different mindset. The experience is generally furtive, secretive, ashamed. While it might be acceptable to mention at the office the next day that you had been to the cinema the night before and watched *Deep Throat,* purely to see what all the fuss was about, naturally, you might think twice before regaling colleagues with the news that you stayed home and masturbated over *Anal Virgins IV.*

Pornography, although more massively distributed than it had ever previously been, was now reduced to a mass market without any standards or criteria, rapidly accumulating an attendant atmosphere of sordidness and shame. Still, just so long as pornographic culture could be kept indoors, a private, addictive, and increasingly expensive vice, it remained a very lucrative commodity. As noted earlier, sexual fantasy is something that is free to anyone still in possession of a sexual imagination, but the pornographic video or DVD sells us a lifeless and lackluster substitute for something we could have created much more satisfyingly ourselves. This, in the eyes of the authorities, must be the perfect situation for pornography: make it available, so that those massive revenues and taxes can start rolling in, but keep it frowned upon and shameful so that you don't get an Allen Ginsberg turning up and claiming that it's art, it's civil liberties, a movement, politics—anything that sounds dangerous.

Of course, both sex and sexual expression are political and always have been, but it wasn't until the late 1960s and the 1970s that they were widely seen as such. Sprung up from the same sixties counterculture that had given rise to Robert Crumb came femi-

Aubrey Beardsley PLATE FROM THE *LYSISTRATA*, 1896

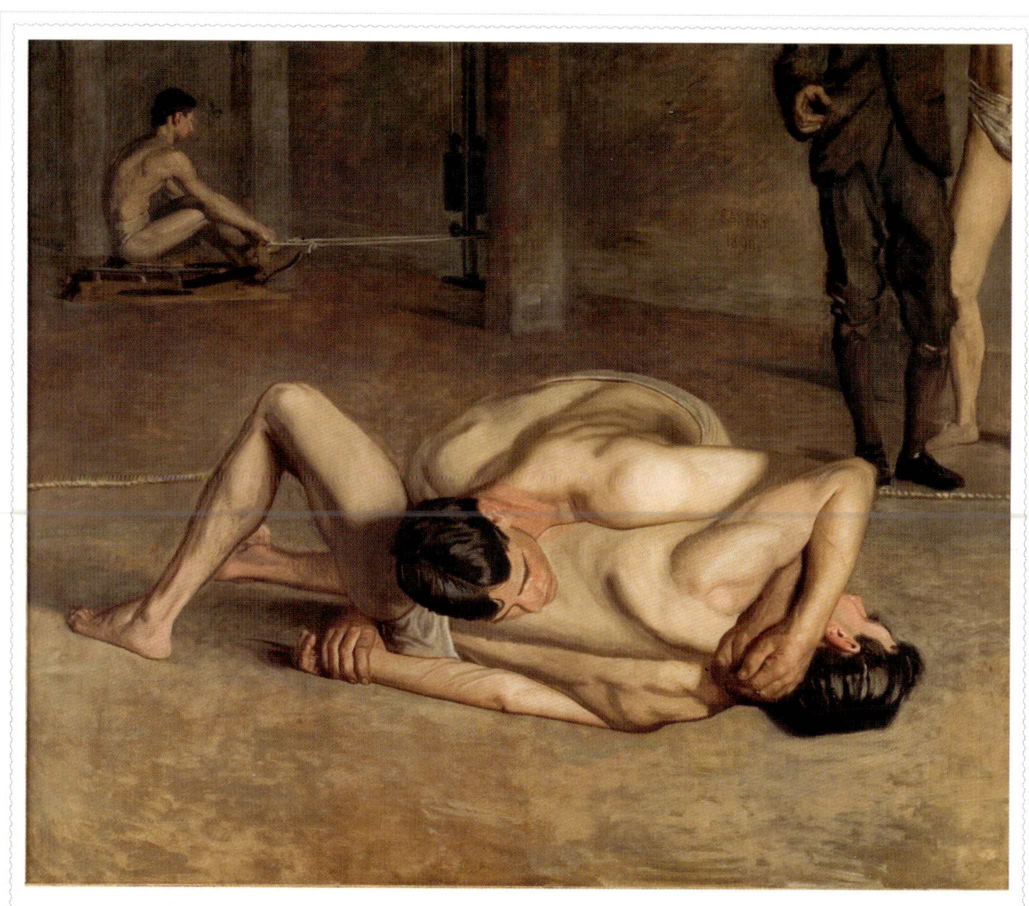

Thomas Eakins WRESTLERS, 1899

nism to provide the artist with his fiercest critics. Feminists took the position that pornography exploited and degraded women, which was certainly an argument that it was difficult to disagree with in light of much of the material that was available around that time. If it had remained just that—an argument put forward as an element in a continuing debate—then it might not have polarized the liberal community to the degree that it unquestionably came to do. Instead of putting ideas forward as a proposition, feminism at the time delivered them as dictums from a moral high ground. And instead of properly considering the issues raised by feminism, liberal men perceived themselves as victims of an unprovoked attack upon their sexuality, responding angrily. Feminist protestors against porn would find themselves uneasy bedfellows with right-wing Christian campaigners and would also find themselves on the receiving end of an equivalent amount of left-wing ire, some of it justified and some of it unfair.

For one thing, it's important to distinguish between the objections of the chanting feminists and those of placard-waving Christians, even when they're part of the same picket line outside an adult video emporium. Feminist arguments, even those one may not agree with, are at least constructed on the principles of logic and therefore can be debated, having precepts that are falsifiable—that can be proved or disproved. Religious arguments against pornography, alternately, are based upon the idea of a disapproving super-being, proof of whose existence has thus far eluded us. This is not to say that God does not exist, nor that religious people aren't entitled to their point of view, but is simply intended to point out that ideas predicated upon a specific deity's existence are not rational ideas, and therefore have no place in rational discussion. I'm sorry, I don't make the rules. That's just the way it is, and we would have to entirely change the meaning of the English language before we could make it otherwise.

Despite the rational basis of the feminist agenda, though, it had been served up, understandably, as confrontation, and high feelings on both sides meant that a sensible debate would never really be a possibility. The already-fragmented Left became divided upon

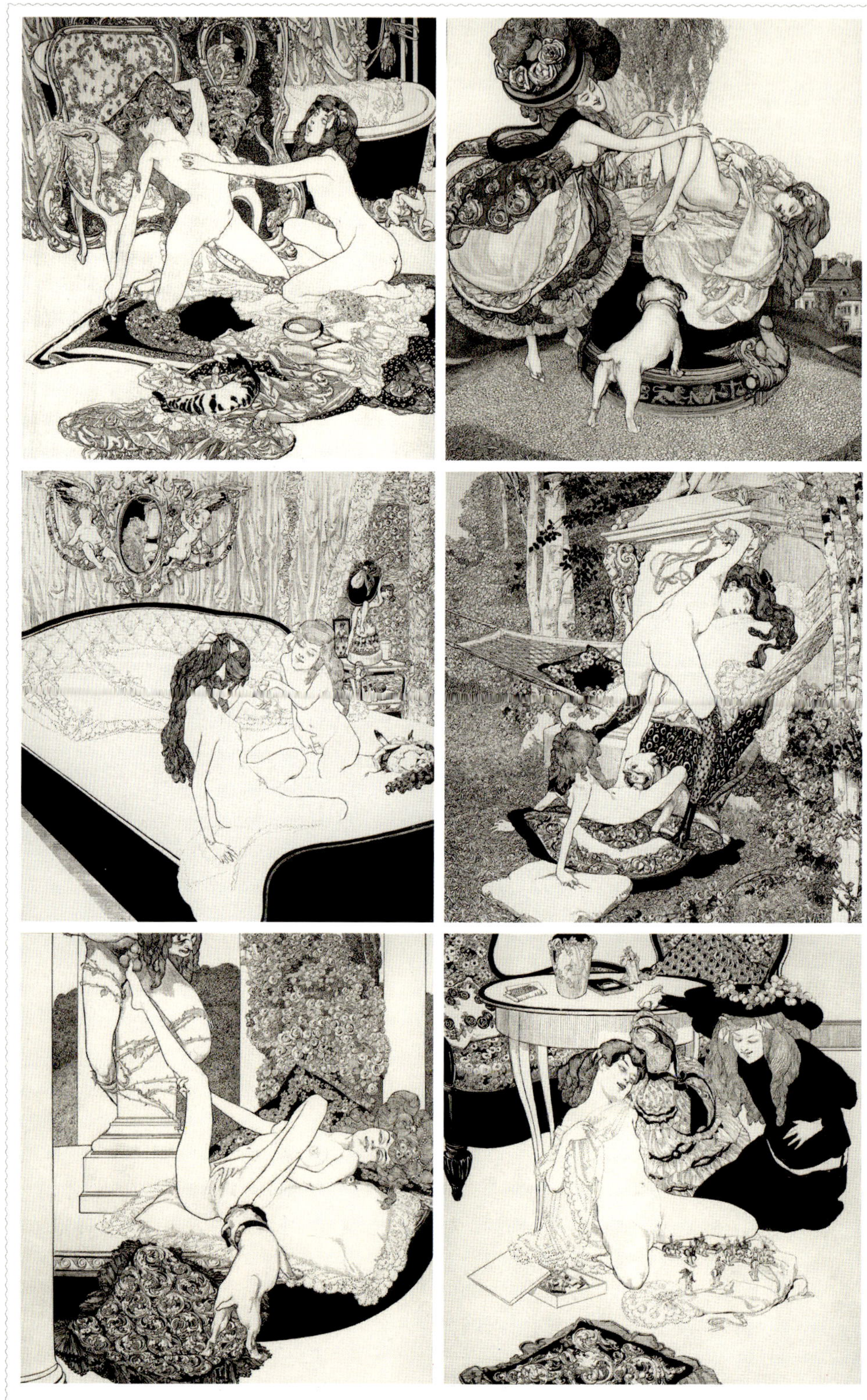

Franz von Bayros ABOVE AND OPPOSITE: *TALES FROM THE DRESSING TABLE*, 1900

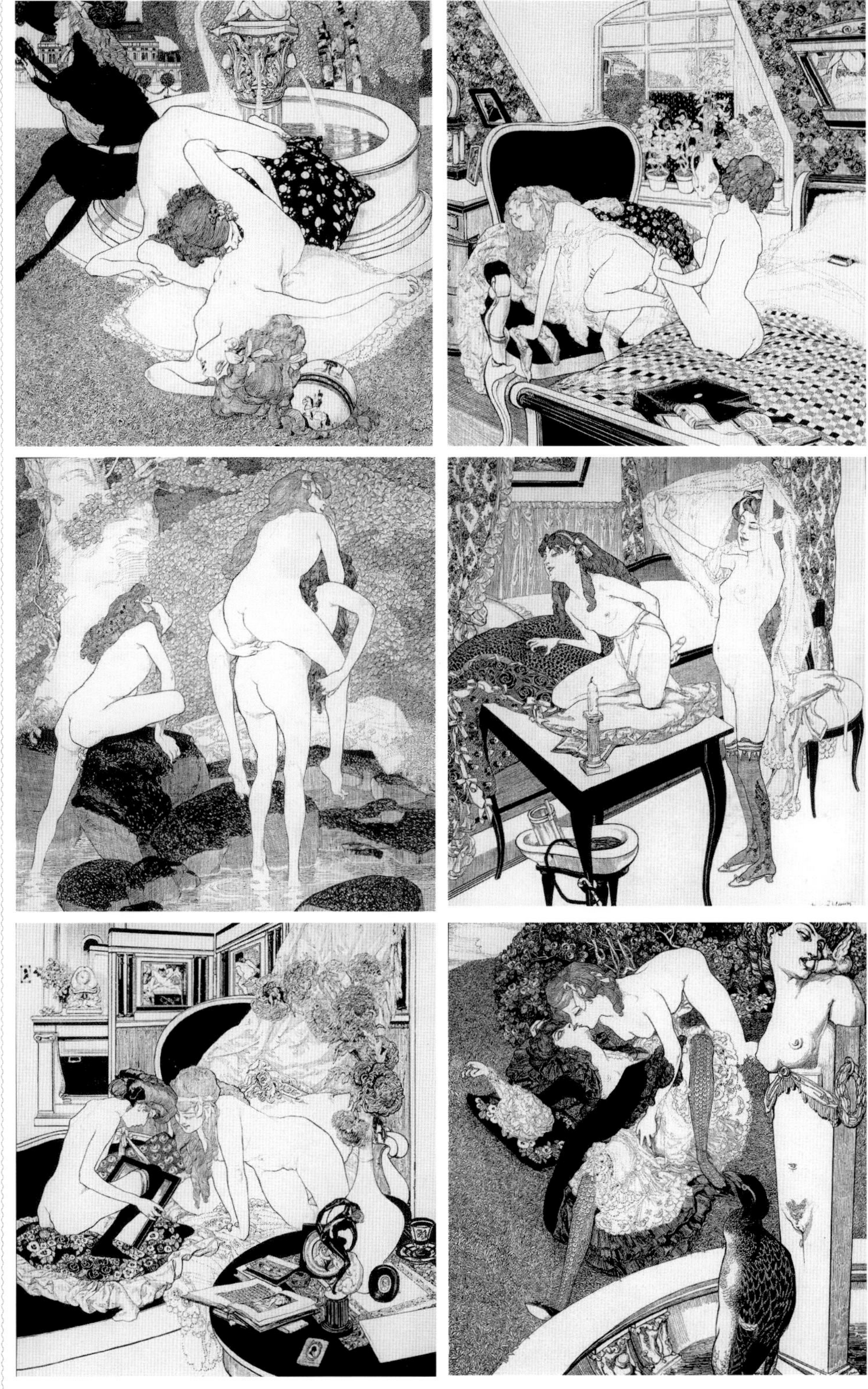

grounds of gender, with both camps in their entrenched and stalemated positions—men insisting that the issue was completely one of civil liberties, women insisting it was one of sexual politics. Both sides were right, of course, but by then were not speaking to each other, so the debate remained in deadlock.

Attitudes toward pornography had not just brought about a schism in the liberal ranks, though, but had pretty much split feminism itself down the middle. Many women, and some men, who still believed that women had a way to go before social equality was reached became reluctant to describe themselves as feminists because of the censorious and illiberal connotations that the term had taken on. Rejecting feminism's dogma on pornography, some women made an effort to reclaim the genre in pro-sexual publications such as *On Our Backs*, its title borrowed impishly from hardline feminist mag *Off Our Backs*. Elsewhere were the first stirrings of the erstwhile network that would later call itself Feminists Against Censorship.

Although it would eventually be these dissenting female voices who would suggest a possible solution to the unproductive stand-off on the issue of pornography, during the mid-nineties the arrival of the Internet would mean that, once more, any ethical debate of the subject would be swept to one side, overtaken by events and by the socially transforming onslaught of technology. Just as home video had meant that porno could be privately enjoyed by a much greater segment of the population, the arrival of the Internet took all that one stage further. Whereas renting videos or DVDs might still entail the risk of being caught by an acquaintance scuttling furtively out of a rental outlet, or of having one's porn stash discovered by a disapproving spouse, the Internet apparently removed that final hurdle. It became clear that a large majority of people weren't as frightened of pornography as they were scared of being found out.

England, in the 1970s, was racked by strikes that culminated in a national three-day week while shops and businesses were closed by power failures. If the blackouts happened unexpectedly, then stores and supermarkets found that there were sudden bursts of opportunist shoplifting. Even at the upmarket retail chains such as Marks & Spencer, managers discovered that their prim, predominantly middle-class customers weren't averse to slipping some expensive item deep within their twinsets when the lights were out. Public morality must obviously be seen to be observed in order to retain one's social standing, but when no one can see anything at all, it's a different matter.

So it was with the arrival of the Internet: In cyberspace, no one can hear you climax. Since reputedly the greater part of all the traffic on this information superhighway is devoted to the viewing or downloading of pornography, we must assume that the demand for porn is almost universal. Perusing smut would seem to be no longer an activity confined to isolated sexual deviants, but more a pastime human beings simply enjoy when left to their own devices. Also it would seem as if commercial porno has become the undiscussed wallpaper of contemporary society—it is so ubiquitous that it is accepted without question as a fact of life.

Pornography, or what would only recently have been referred to as pornography, is now a part of mainstream culture. Having sexual undertones or even overtones since its inception, pop music during the 1980s first began to consciously adopt overtly pornographic stances with a repertoire of pornographic imagery and references employed by artists such as Prince, Madonna, Frankie Goes to Hollywood, and a parade of others. Where Chuck Berry had been banned for serving up single-entendres on the subject of his ding-a-ling, and Lou Reed got away with Candy Darling giving head in his "Walk on the Wild Side" solely because British censors didn't understand the term, the Spice Girls now convey their need to *Zig-a-zig-ahh* to an audience of ten-year-old girls with complete impunity.

Properly packaged as a taxable commodity, erotic imagery pervades our culture to an extent that would have been previously unimaginable. While pornography employed by individuals for their personal pleasure as an aid to masturbation is still seen as

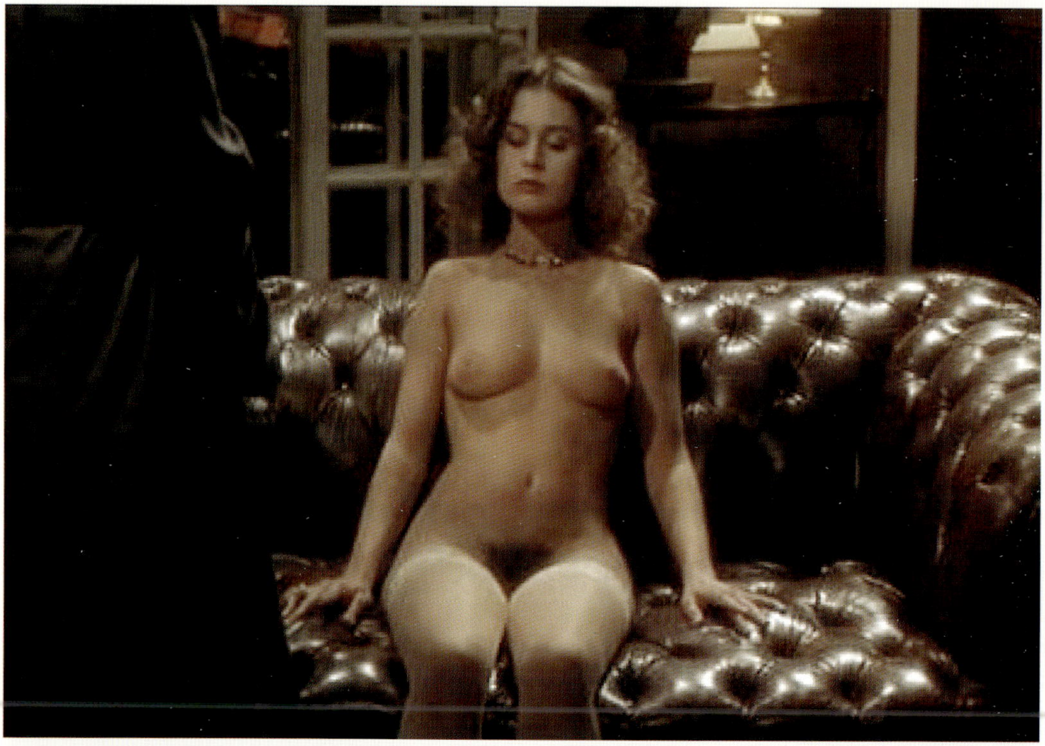

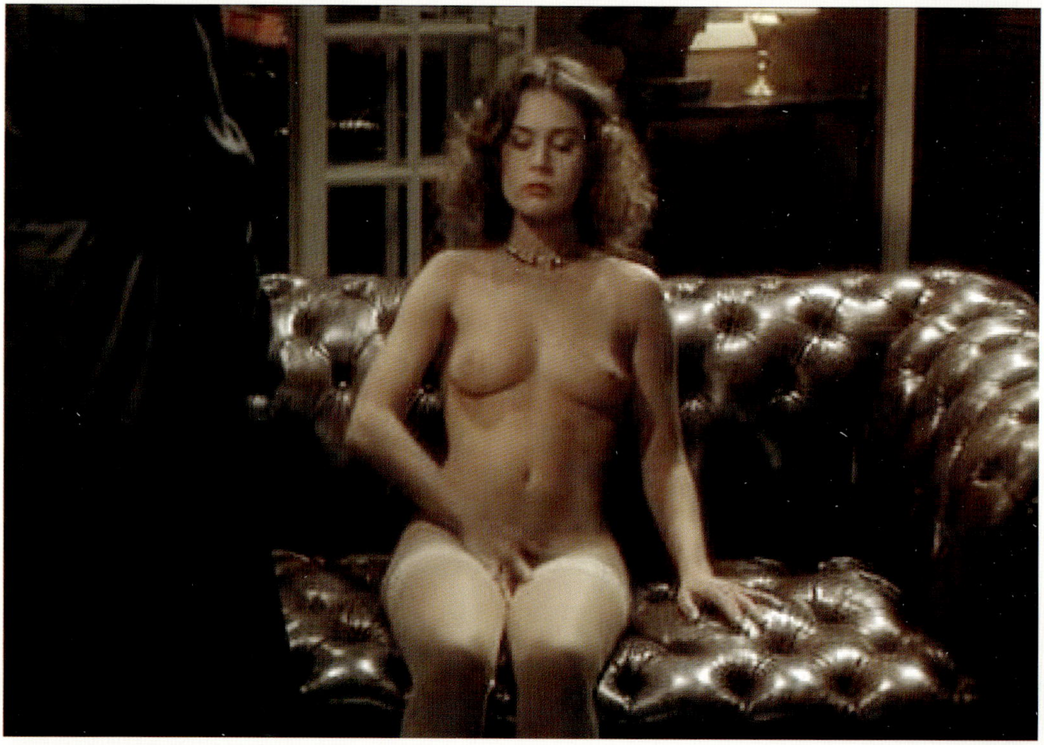

something vaguely shameful, its use in a corporate context, as a means of selling us consumer goods, is smiled on. Advertisers fill our television screens and billboards with it, trying to associate their snack food, car, or line of sweaters with arousal so that they can shift more units. Rock, pop, and rap promoters drape their artists' videos and lyrics in it without comment, so that in a climate of increased concern and indeed mounting panic over pedophilia it's perfectly OK for Britney Spears to posture in a fetishistic schoolgirl outfit of a type that cannot actually have been worn by a schoolgirl any time this century. The word "fuck," once inflammatory when on the lips of Allen Ginsberg, Lenny Bruce, or Kenneth Tynan, can be cutely scrambled as the logo for the French Connection clothing line's United Kingdom franchise. The big difference between our commercial porno-culture and traditional pornography, however, is that while the former is more limited and soft-core than the latter, it's no longer something sought out by an eager and consenting individual but instead is a feature of society that there is no avoiding—it's there whether we like it or not. As a culture, we are more intensely sexualized and stimulated than we've ever been before, and from the rising rate of sex crime it appears that we're not dealing with it very well.

Is this because, as Christian moralists and even some unreconstructed feminists might still suggest, pornography corrupts the moral fiber of its victims to the point where fantasies spill over into actual rape or sexual abuse? Probably not, if one considers for a moment just how many people are exposed to pornographic imagery at some point in their lives, and just how tiny a percentage of those people ever have recourse to rape or other sexual crimes. While serial murderers and rapists such as Ted Bundy might claim on the eve of execution that it was pornography that gave them the idea for all their crimes and misdemeanours, this ignores the fact that for each psychopath who makes this claim there are a hundred thousand normal people who appear to never have been pushed over the edge into monstrosity by anything they watched or read. Besides, I've personally yet to find a pornographic work that features anyone removing all their car's interior door handles or dressing in a plaster cast to lull their prey into a false sense of

Just Jaeckin FILM STILLS FROM *THE STORY OF O*, 1975

Larry Clark OVERLEAF: *UNTITLED*, 1972

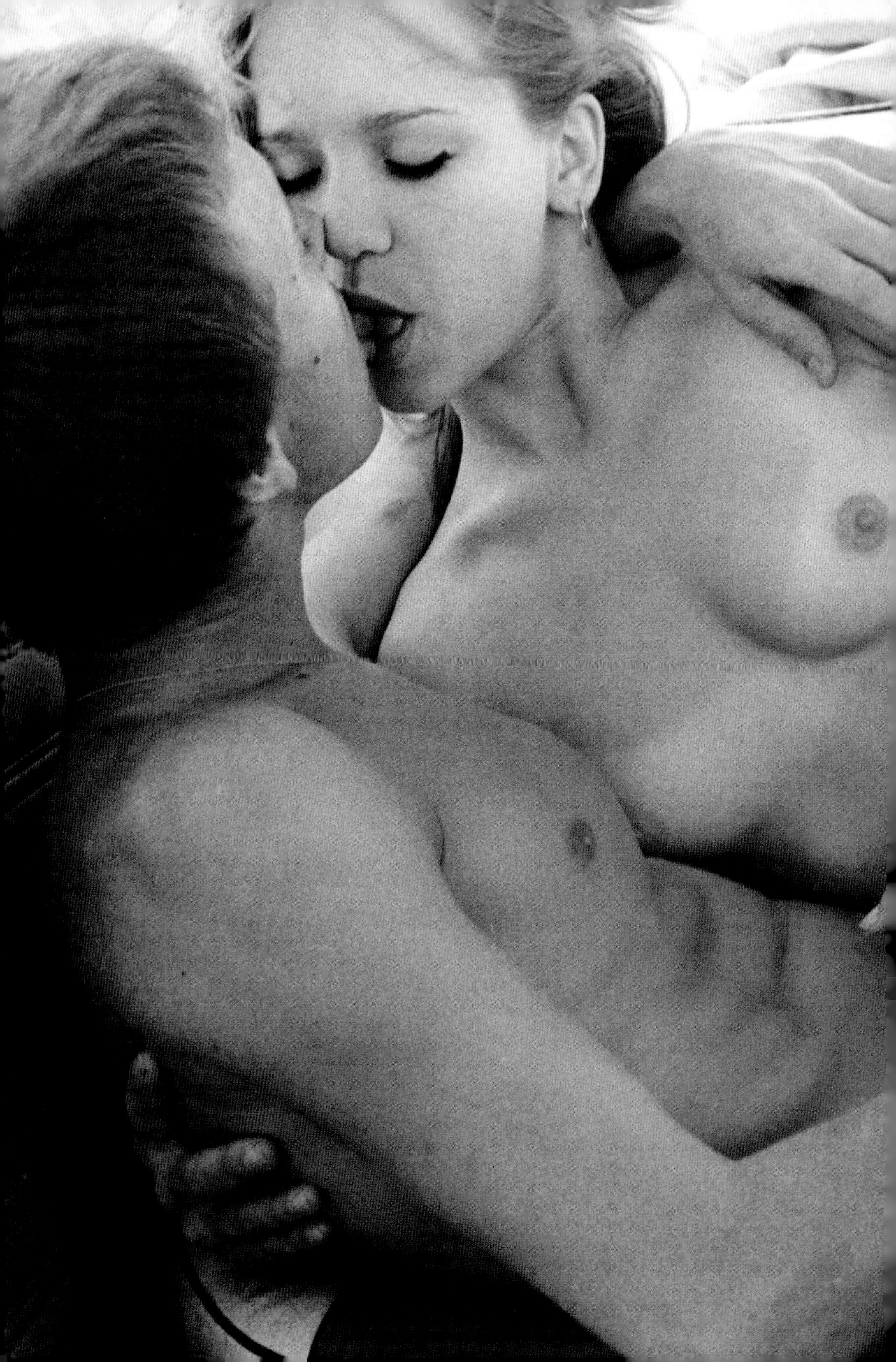

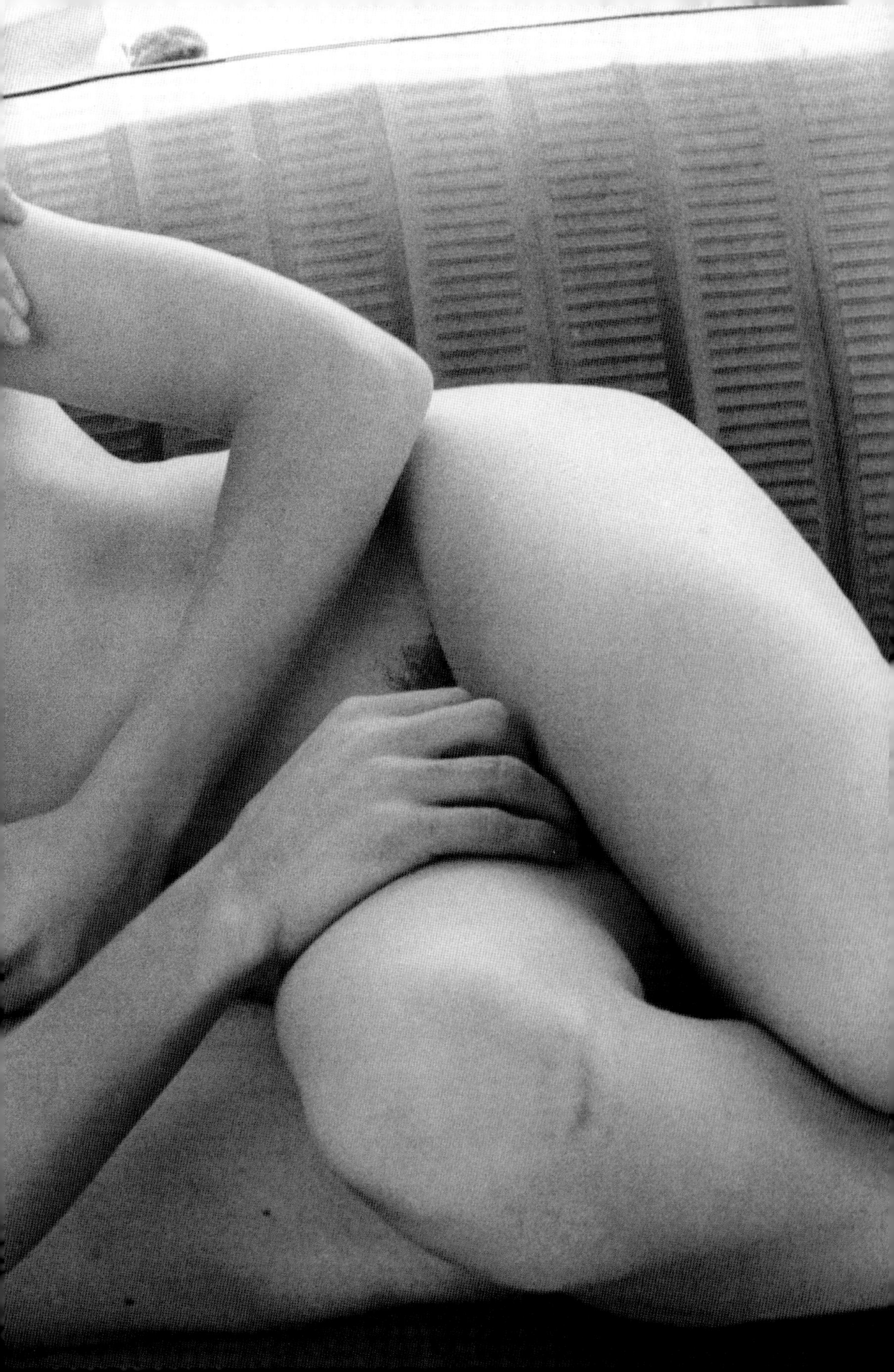

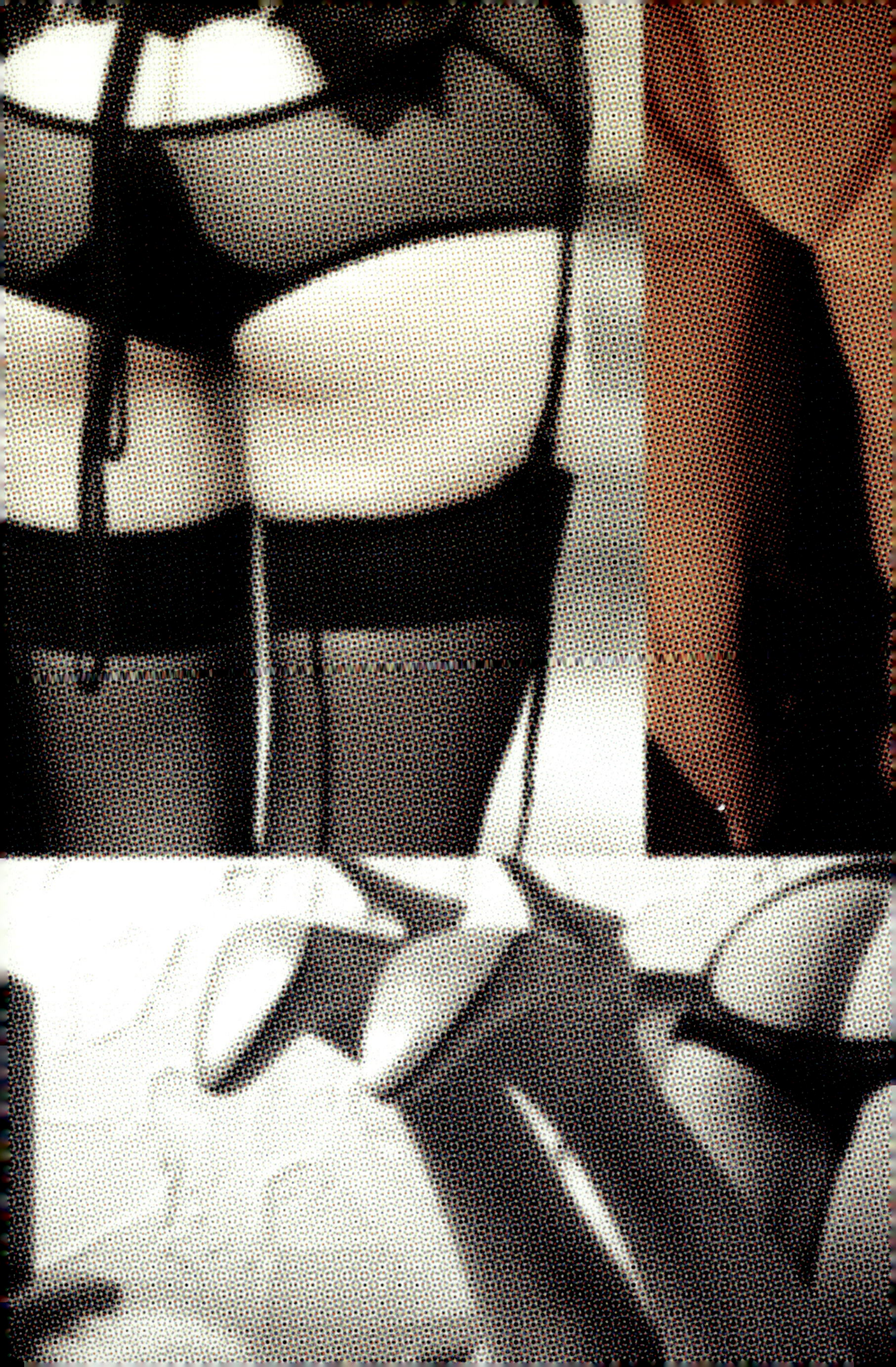

security. Perhaps it's a niche market that I've yet to come across, or possibly those ideas came out of the perpetrator's own psychopathology, not from pornography at all.

Should we decide, then, that there's no connection between the eroticism saturating western culture and the rising tide of sex crime in that culture? Probably, once more, we shouldn't, although the connection may not be as simple and direct as we're expecting. It's instructive to consider different countries in the light of their reaction to pornography, where it appears that the problem might not be in our pornography itself so much as in the way we view pornography as a society. In Denmark, Spain, and Holland it is possible to find hardcore pornography in almost every family newsstand, such fare having become so commonplace that it is barely noticed. With pornography accepted as a fact of life, the attached sense of shame and guilt we find in the United States and Britain is conspicuously absent. Also notable in the porn-tolerant cultures mentioned above is the low rate of sex crime, relative to the United Kingdom and United States, that these cultures enjoy, almost as if within such cultures porno is able to function as a social safety valve in a way that English/American society does not allow. Given that the Internet is global, it's not that these places have less or more porn than we do, nor that they're less sexualized by general culture than ourselves. Could it be, simply, that like Palaeolithic fetish-worshippers or Ancient Greeks, they treat it differently and are affected by it differently in turn?

Consider how we treat pornography on either side of the Atlantic: living in cultures that have been deliberately sexualized for purposes of commerce, it is not unlikely that some of the population will find themselves overstimulated and will seek release from this condition, usually by resorting to whatever form of porno is most readily available. Unfortunately, in societies that have followed the early church's lead by letting people view pornography on the sole understanding that to do so is a sin, such a release will be accompanied almost immediately by a reflex reaction of guilt, shame, embarrassment, and maybe even actual self-disgust.

William Curtis COLLAGE, 2008

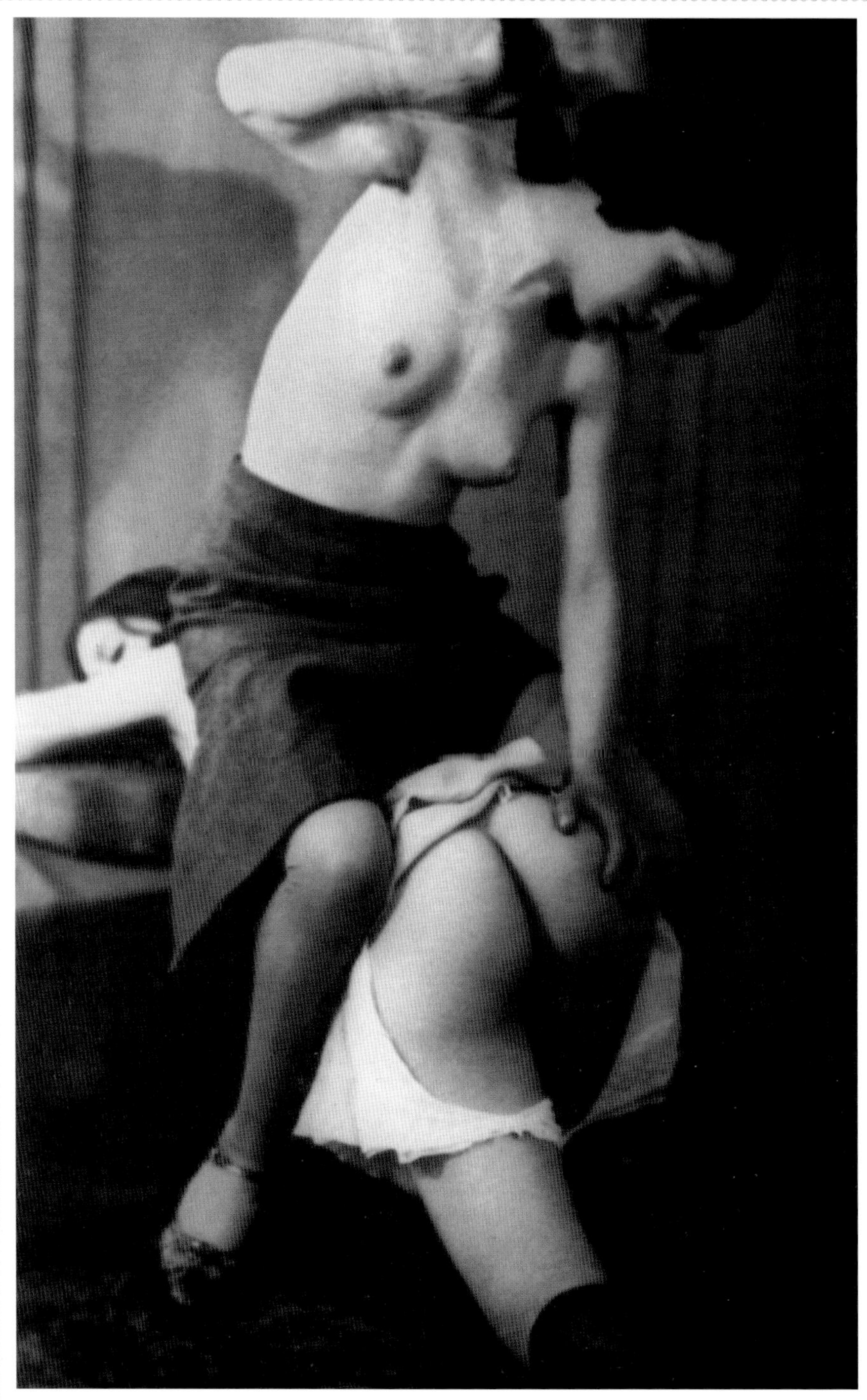

Anonymous VINTAGE DAGUERREOTYPE OF FRENCH *FILLE DE JOIE*, CIRCA 1870

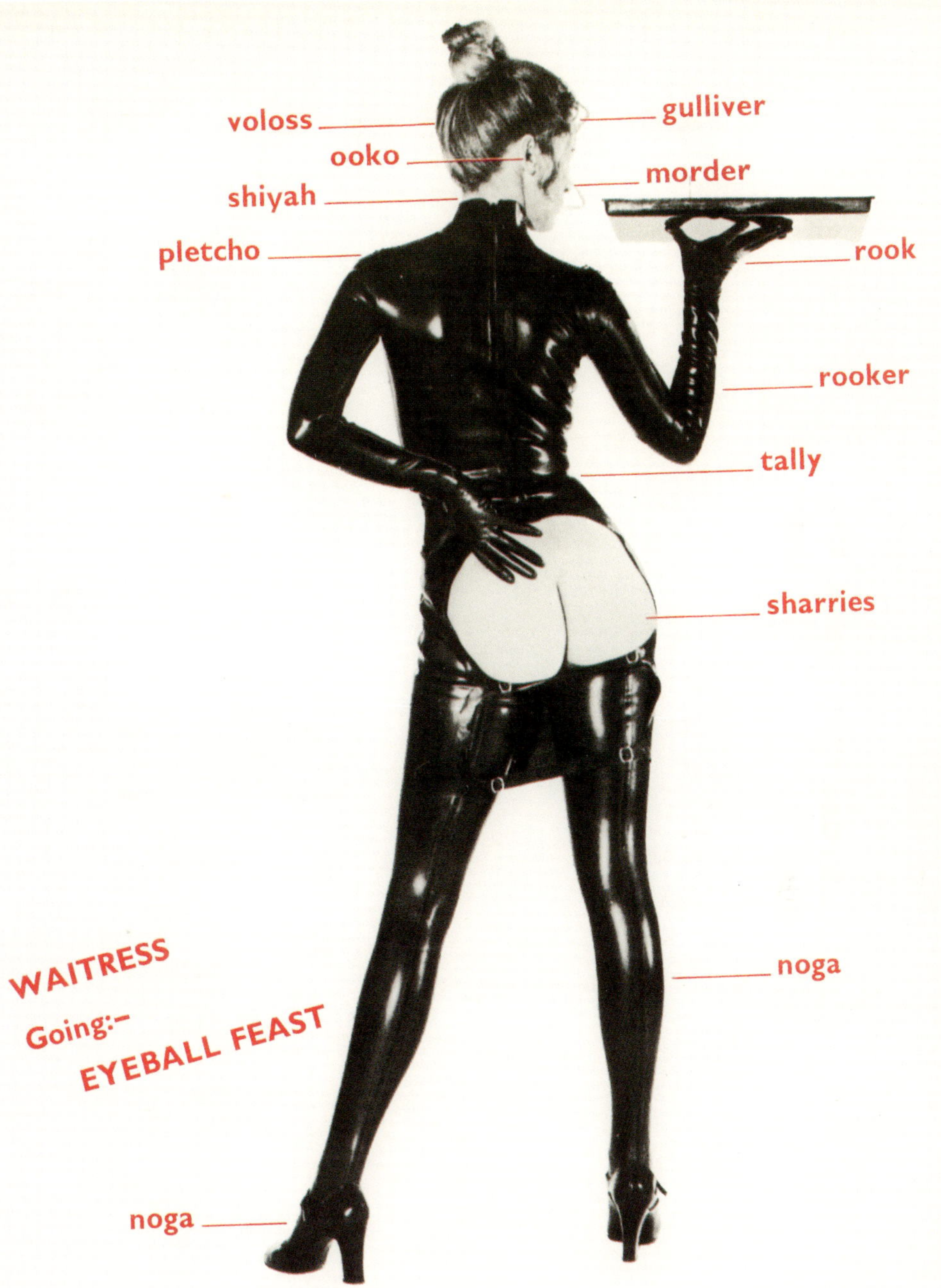

Allen Jones KOROVA MILK BAR WAITRESS UNIFORM FROM STANLEY KUBRICK'S *A CLOCKWORK ORANGE*, 1971

To understand how this conflicted situation could conceivably affect an individual's hard-wiring, let's imagine one of psychologist B. F. Skinner's rat experiments, albeit one that's even more perverse than usual. In our new experiment, the rat is given first his stimulus by means of, say, that schoolgirl promo-piece by Britney Spears we mentioned earlier. Stimulated thus, our rodent is conditioned to respond by pressing on the porno-lever to achieve the requisite reward of sexual release. Once this reward has been acquired, however, our rat will receive a strong electric shock of shame. Reward and punishment, therefore, become perversely linked. The only route to pleasure involves pain and humiliation. Would this treatment, carried out millions of times across whole rodent populations, have a beneficial or a deleterious effect upon their mental health, do you suppose?

With human beings, in the socially constructed Skinner boxes of our sexuality, it isn't going too far to suggest that certain individuals are thus deprived of the release they seek, unable to accept the shame and loathing by which it is accompanied. Extended over an entire society, this means the pressure cooker lid is kept securely on, while the release-valve isn't functioning the way it does in Holland, Spain, or Denmark.

Subsequently we are subjected to more frequent and disastrous explosions of the sex drive—ugly eruptions into real life by what should have been a harmless fantasy. The outcast status of pornography appears to drive some people into shadowy and claustrophobic isolation where their sexual daydreams can turn into something dark and dangerous that is to nobody's advantage, neither themselves, their victims, nor society at large. Worse still, in sexually restrictive cultures where pornography is seen as causing sexual crime (rather than as providing an escape-valve that might possibly prevent it) the instinctual response is almost certainly a fresh attempt to bear down on the pressure-cooker's lid.

Where does this leave us, and where does it leave pornography? With each new technological advance since William Caxton it would seem pornography has both proliferated and degraded in its quality. Today's society, thanks to the Internet and other factors, is entirely saturated with erotica of the most basic, rudimentary kind: convict pornography for convict populations shuffling through life's mess-hall, without any other options than the slop they're given. Porn is everywhere, just as it was in ancient Greece, but where is it in art? Rarely is it an affirmation of common humanity the way it was in classic culture but instead affirms only our alienation and our distance from each other. Despite its mass availability, it does not appear to be making us any happier.

Rather than functioning as a release for our quite ordinary sexual imaginings, porn functions as another social tether, as control-leash, lure, and lash combined in one, a cattle-prod that looks just like a carrot. Dangling temptingly before us everywhere we look, it leads us on. Then, in the guilty aftermath of our indulgences, it converts handily into a rod of shame with which to flog ourselves.

This is especially true of the United States as it negotiates the effects of its own "Georgian" era, although as with the unreasonable influence Victorian England had upon the world back in the nineteenth century, the repercussions of former faith-based presidencies in America are felt across the globe. They're felt in terms of their effect on foreign policy, on the sciences and arts, and on how we think about our sexuality and its entitlements. Soaking in cyber-porn and promo-porn, the sexual heat within society is higher than it's ever been—the needle on the boiler's dial tipping alarmingly into the red—yet at this point in history we're governed by a mindset that is programmed to respond by clamping down on the escape valve, on pornography. Wipe out pornography, the idea seems to be, and we'll have also somehow wiped out all the urges that first prompted us to sculpt Bog Venus in the first place.

Clearly, the eradication of pornography is never going to happen. Porn's been with us since our Palaeolithic past and will in every likelihood be with us until we succeed in tidying our species from the planet. "No porn," then, is not a realistic option. I suggest that the only choice we genuinely have is between good pornography and bad pornography. This obviously begs a bunch of questions,

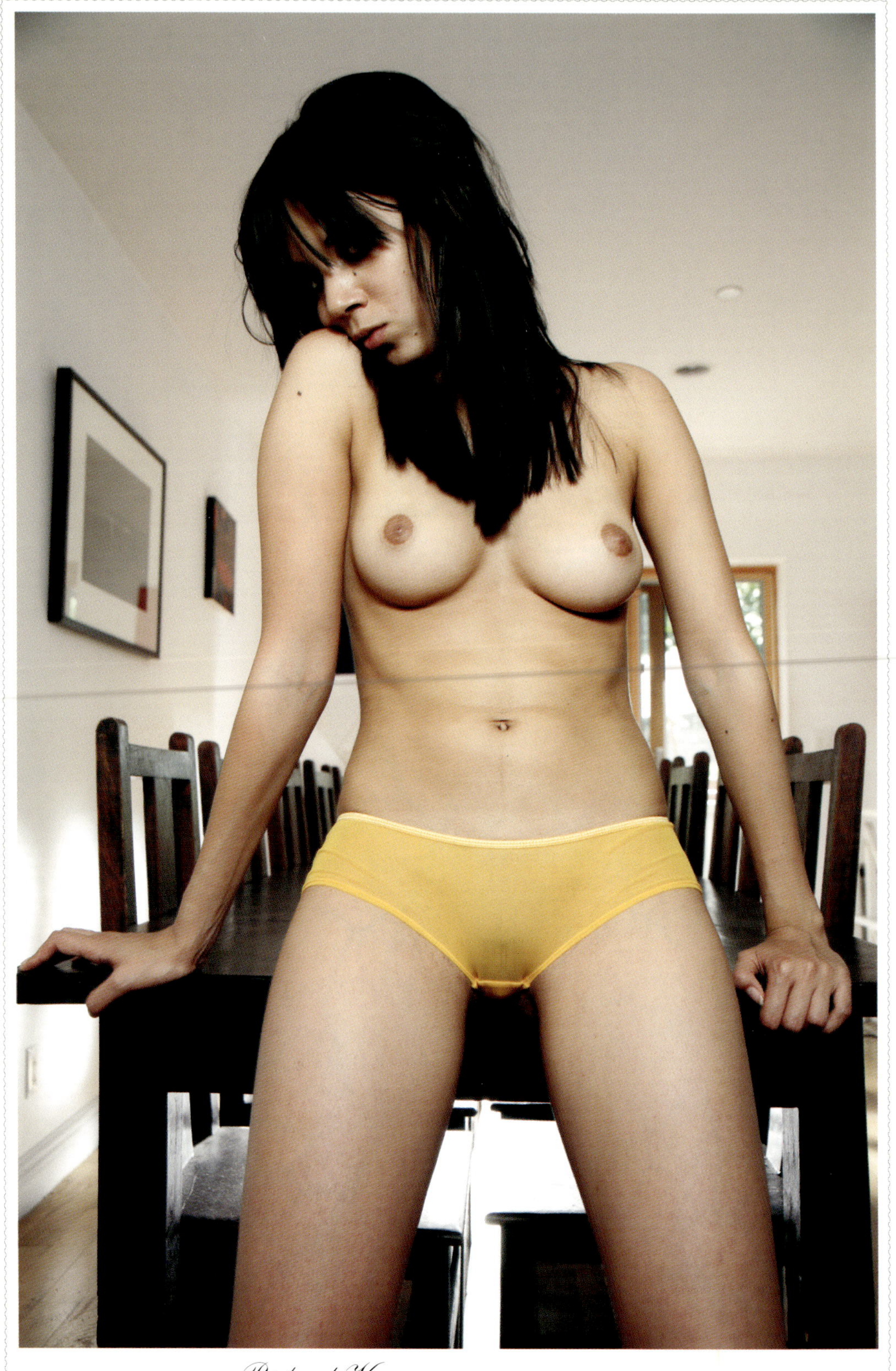

Richard Kern MAISSA IN YELLOW PANTIES, 2005

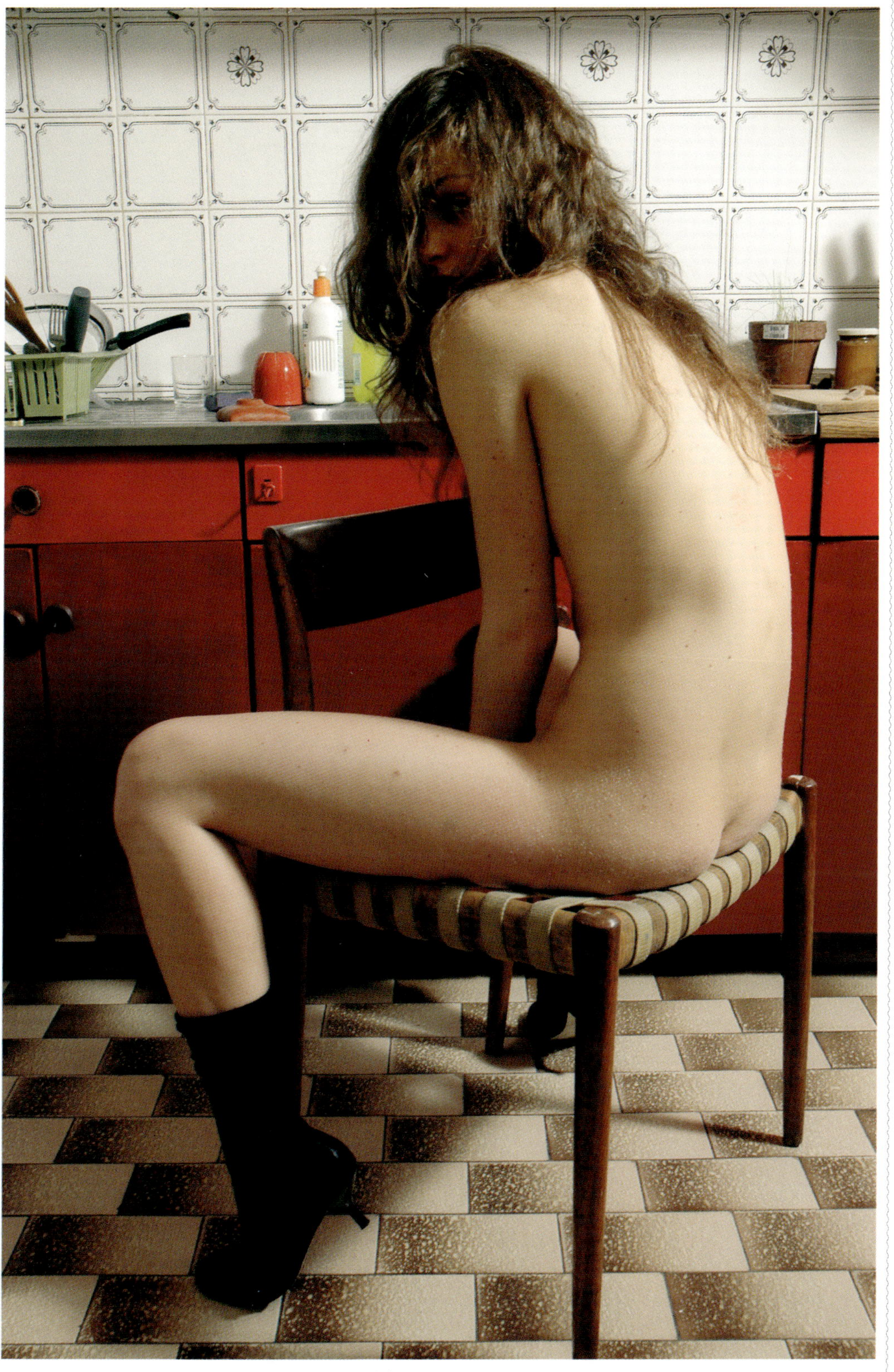

Richard Kern GABBY IN THE KITCHEN, 2004

the first being how we differentiate between the two. Just for the purposes of argument let us define "good" porn, like good Judge Clayton Horn, as that which is of noticeable social benefit, with "bad" porn as its opposite, that which is noticeably to our social detriment. Of course, this raises a much bigger question, namely, does "good" porn even exist? If not, could it conceivably exist at some point in the future, and what would it look like if it did?

To answer this, we could do far worse than refer back to those few dissenting female voices that were raised, back when the feminist debate upon pornography was at its hottest and perhaps its most intelligent. Taking some inspiration from Simone de Beauvoir's influential essay *Must We Burn Sade?*, the wonderful and greatly missed Angela Carter muses on porn in her book *The Sadeian Women*, finally suggesting that there might be some form of pornography yet undiscovered, glorious and liberating, unencumbered by the inequalities of sex and sexuality that dogged it in the past. Even porn's most uncompromising and vociferous feminist critic, Andrea Dworkin, has conceded that benign pornography might be conceivable, even if she considered such a thing highly unlikely. Given that we don't want "bad" pornography and can't have no pornography, it's in this mere suggestion of the possibility of "good" pornography that the one ray of light in an intractable debate resides.

The question still remains, however, how pornography might have a beneficial influence upon society, exactly? If we can't imagine such a situation, then how would we recognize it if it should arise? Even if we agree with Andrea Dworkin, Angela Carter, Kathy Acker, and Simone de Beauvoir that our hypothetical "good" porn is possible, that doesn't help us much unless we have a clear idea of just what good, what benefit, pornography of the right kind might work within our culture.

We've observed already that in places such as Denmark, Spain, or Holland porn appears to act to some extent as a release valve, venting sexual pressures harmlessly before they can explode in sex crime or abuse. We also noted that this doesn't seem to work in more restrictive cultures, where reflexive guilt and shame seem to attend the very notion of pornography. What if it were possible to bring such a degree of artistry to our pornography that this immediate link between erotica and dire social embarrassment was severed? Might pornography in this way be allowed to function as it does in more enlightened climes, reducing our appalling score of actual men and women scarred and violated, actual children raped and killed and dumped in a canal? Isn't such a thing at least worth the attempt? Pornography, if it could be expressed artistically in such a way, might welcome our sexual imagination in from the cold, into the reassuring warmth of socio-political acceptability. The power of art is that it lets us see, in someone else's work, an idea that we dimly formed but lacked the skill to realize or convey, and in this way makes us feel less alone. Pornography as we conceive of it today, however, does the opposite. It isn't art, cannot be openly admired or discussed, and serves only to convince us of our isolation, to increase our sense that we are in our secret and most intimate desires alone save for the reeking company of other sweaty, masturbating perverts and social inadequates.

If we could redefine erotica, restore it to the venerated place in art that it was once accustomed to, this might defuse a number of our personal and social tensions with regard to sex in much the way it seems to have done at the dawn of western civilization. Realized properly, pornography could offer us a safe arena in which to discuss or air ideas that otherwise would go unspoken and could only fester in our individual dark. Our sexual imagination is and always has been central to our lives, as individuals or as a species, and our culture might be much enriched, or at least more relaxed, if it acknowledged this. There'd be no more divine pornography by any future William Blake incinerated after his demise, no future Aubrey Beardsley on his deathbed, frightened, coughing for his finest work to be destroyed, no frilly decadent or bearded Beat compelled either to cower behind a pseudonym or add to the prolific oeuvre of "Anonymous."

Ennobled thus, pornography could take its place once more as a revered and almost sacred totem in society—could be brought full

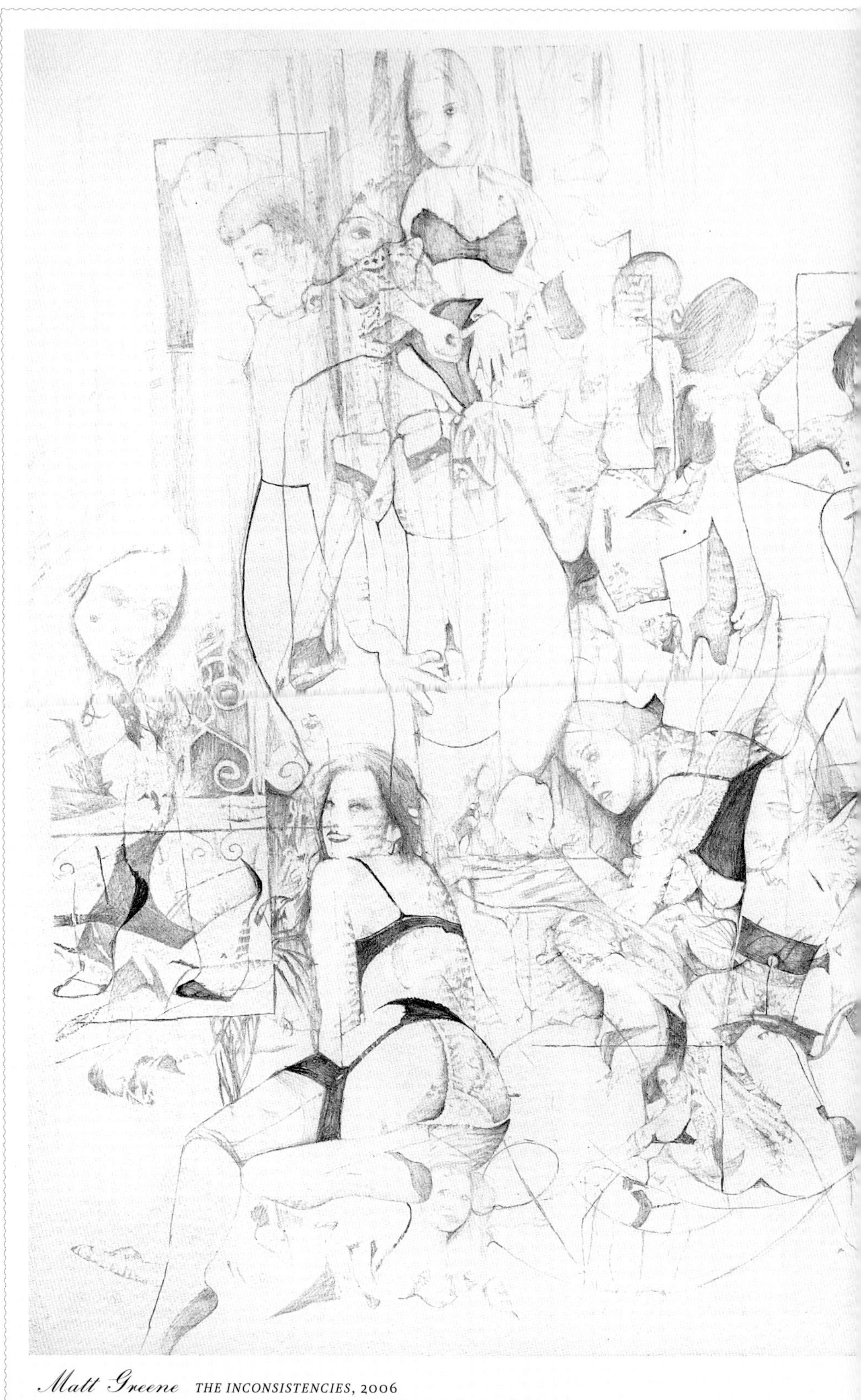

Matt Greene *THE INCONSISTENCIES*, 2006

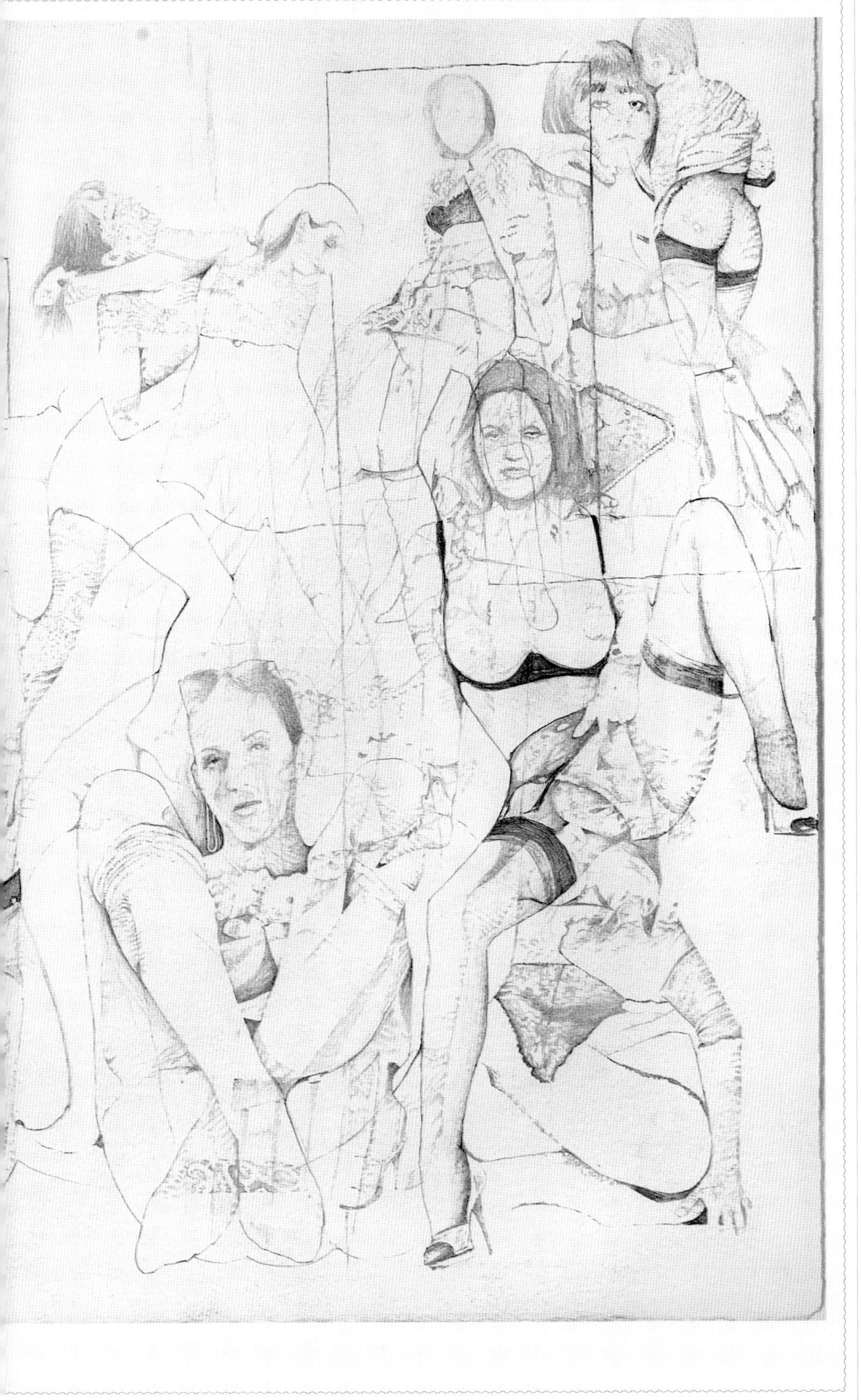

circle to its origins in the pneumatic pinhead babe of Willendorf. It seems we only have two choices in the way that we regard our own erotic dreams: either we can accept them and restore Bog Venus to her natural and proper place in culture, or we can reject them and attempt to stigmatize them, attaching arousal to so much conditioned shame and guilt and pain that in effect we have contained our sexuality within a spiky nineteenth-century German cockring.

In the end, it is in the hands of individual people—individual artists, writers, filmmakers, or poets. If they have the nerve to plant their flags in this despised and dangerous terrain despite its uninviting nature, then in time the dismal wilderness might be transformed into a scented garden of enduring value. The erotic might be elevated from her current status as a hooker everyone keeps chained up in their cellar but nobody talks about, unmentionable but available, back to her previous position as a goddess.

We might find she's changed some since her chunky limestone origins, might find she now resembles something more along the lines depicted in *Pornokrates* by the magnificent Félicien Rops. This superb work, begun by Rops in the late 1870s, depicts the spirit of pornography herself, a gorgeous woman seen in profile treading carefully from right to left across the image, clad in only boots, gloves, stockings, jewelry, and a drifting sash, topped by a Gainsborough hat. Pale flowers are in her hair, and, similarly pale, there is a blindfold tied across her eyes. Held on a leash as though it were a well-clipped poodle is a lean young pig that seems to lead the sightless beauty in the manner of a guide dog. At a pace sedate and dignified, it navigates for its blind mistress what may be only a decorative lower border to the picture but which looks like the embellished stonework of a wall or ledge, along the top of which the elegant embodied spirit of Victorian pornography is guided by a snuffling hog; a swine before the pearl.

A frieze runs in relief along the wall or border's topmost edge, depicting effigies of the fine arts, seated with their parchment, lute,

---

Félicien Rops *PORNOKRATES*, 1878

Vanessa Beecroft OVERLEAF: *VB45*, 2001

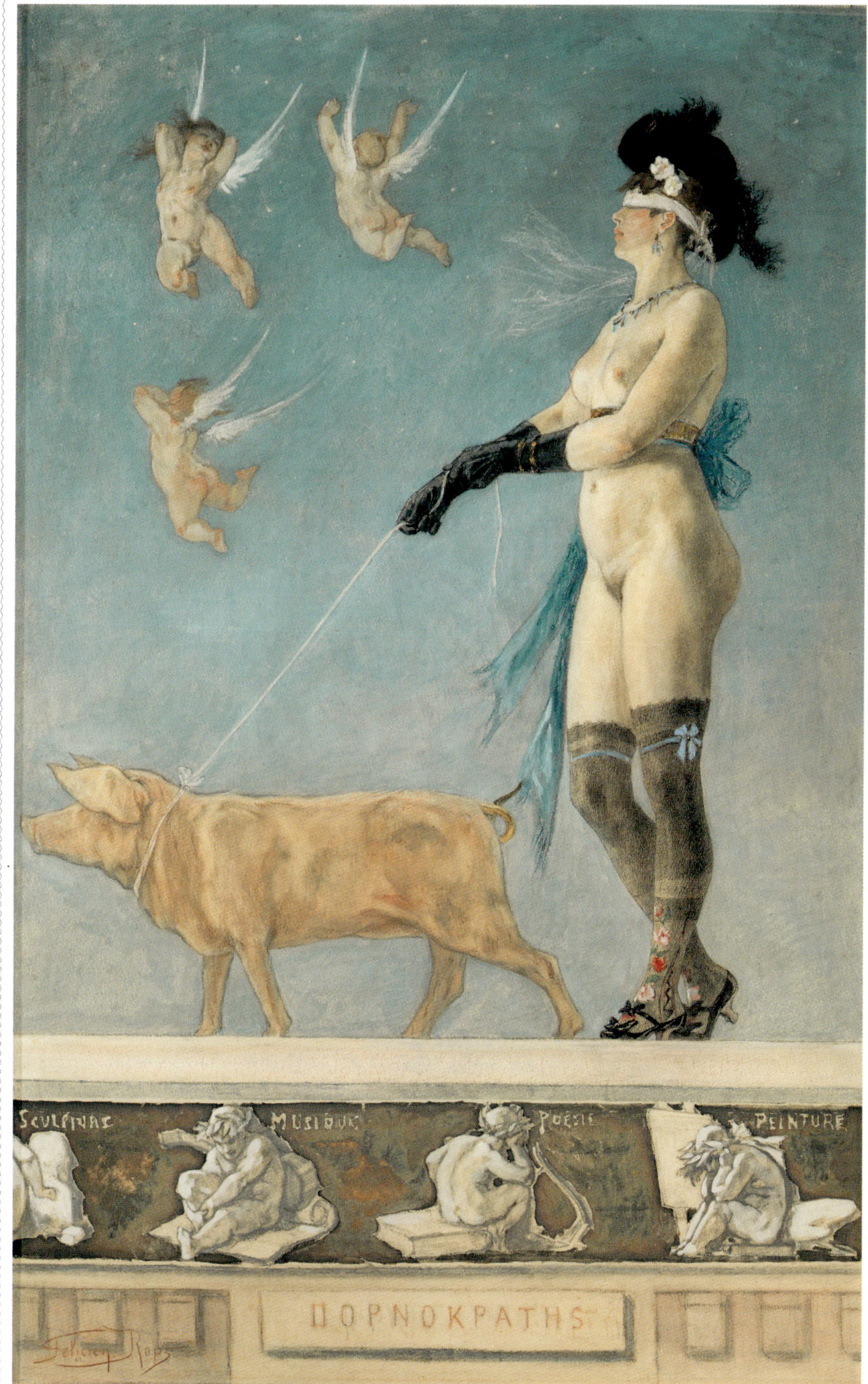
SCULPTURE
MUSIQUE
POESIE
PEINTURE
ΠOPNOKPATHS
Félicien Rops

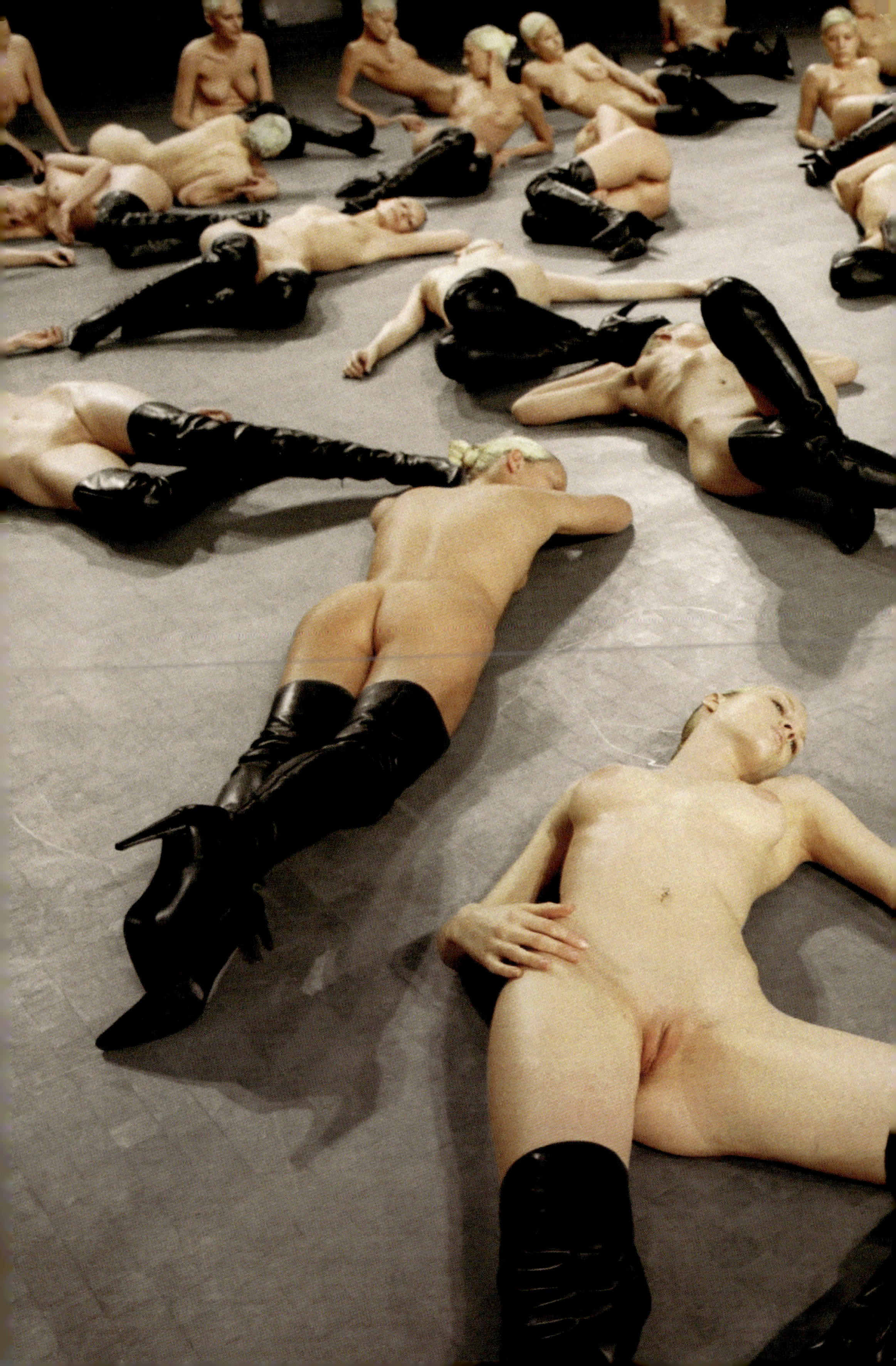

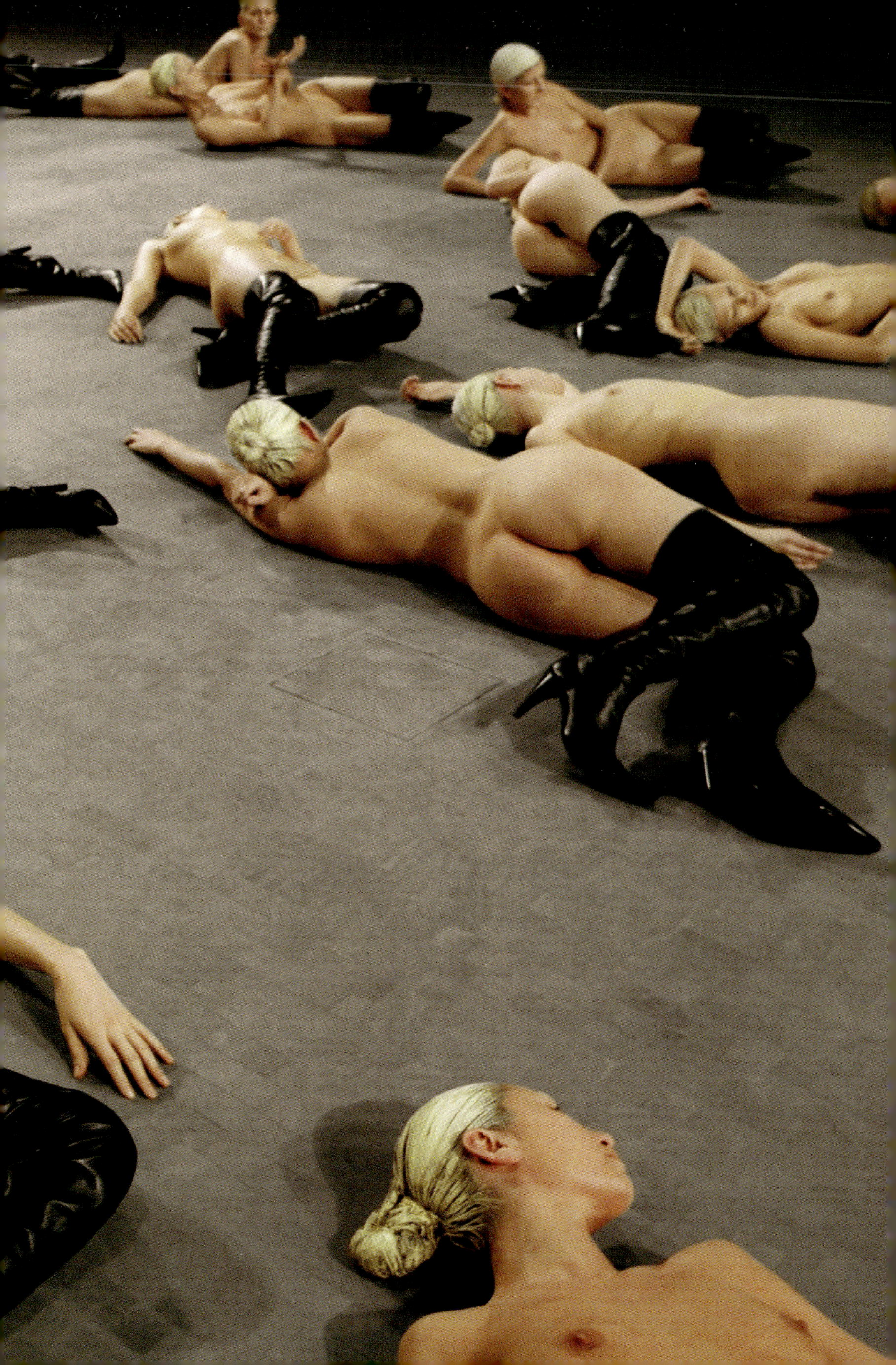

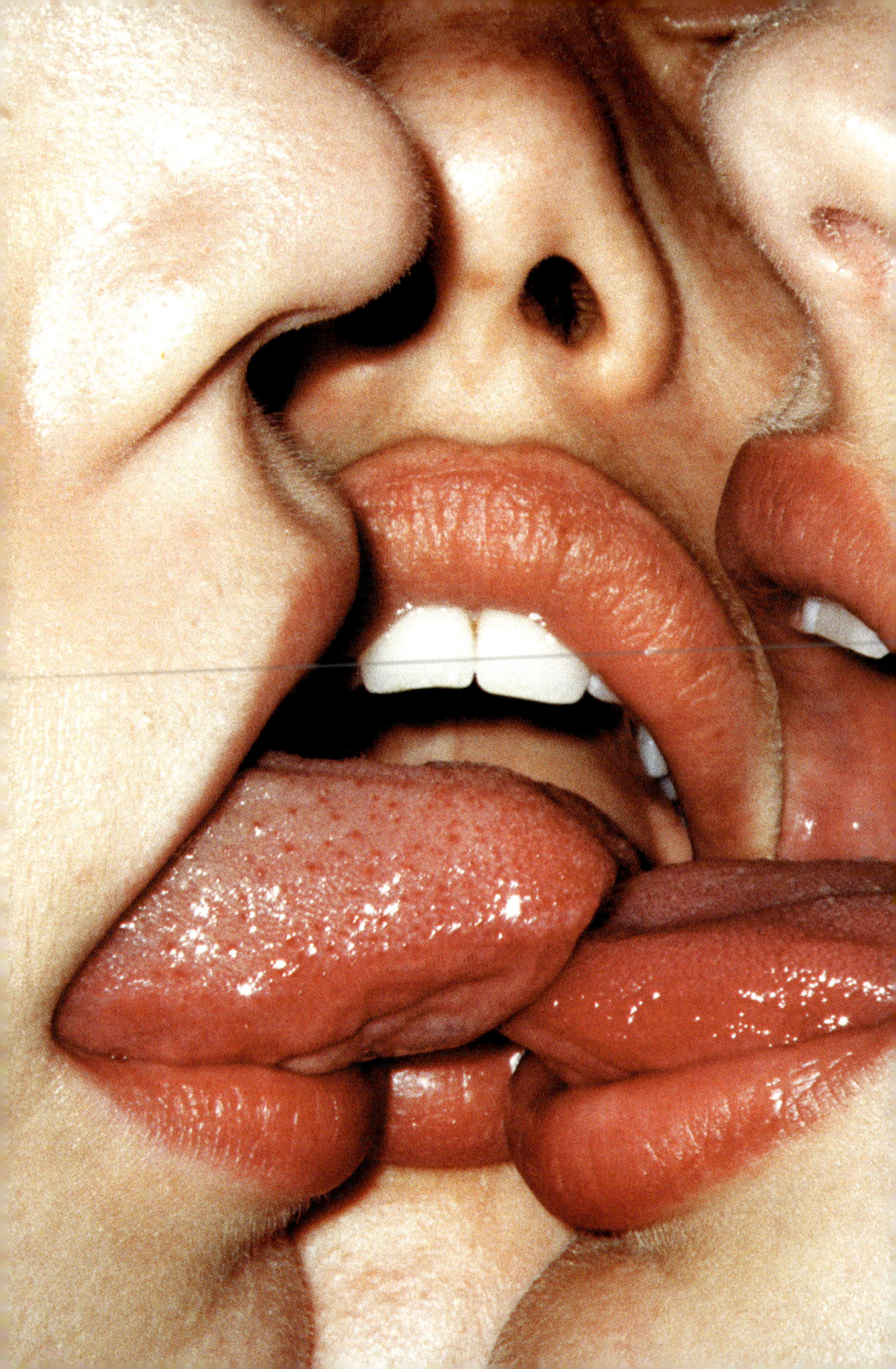

or easel and yet hanging down their heads, looking away embarrassed as the goddess of pornography parades there brazenly above them. Similarly, hovering in the air before her as she walks there are three anguished cherubs, tearing at their hair as they regard her lewd display. Behind her blindfold, unaware of how she looks and rightly unconcerned by the controversy she's causing, utterly unworried by the precipice she steps along, the voluptuous essence of pornography is calm, serene. She trusts her safety to an animal conventionally seen as the epitome of dirtiness and brutish instinct, this despite its widely mentioned cleanliness and keen intelligence. The goddess walks along her wall, proud and unmindful of the drop to either side, secure in her conviction that she is a thing of loveliness, safe in the knowledge that by following her noble and yet much-despised animal urge she will be led unerringly toward her rightful queenly destiny.

Shameless and blind to all the outraged posturings occasioned by her presence, Venus promenades along the moral tightrope of her path, walking the pig, sure-footed and invulnerable in her glamour as she wanders, one step at a time, toward the hoped-for glow of a more human and enlightened future.

Terry Richardson UNTITLED, 2007

Page 1. Vintage daguerreotype of French *fille de joie*, circa 1870. Courtesy private collection.

Page 4. Vintage French postcard, early 1900s. Courtesy private collection.

Page 8. Vintage daguerreotype of French *fille de joie*, circa 1870. Courtesy private collection.

Page 11. *Venus of Willendorf*, Oolitic limestone, 4.38 in. (11.1 cm). Courtesy of Naturhistorische Museum, Wien, Austria. Photograph © Ali Meyer, the Bridgeman Art Library.

Page 12. Devi Jagamandi from the Temple at Khajuraho, Madhya. Courtesy the Association for World Heritage Sites in India.

Page 15. Athenian Lovers, bowl. Fifth century B.C., from the Antiquities and Cast Gallery. Courtesy The Ashmolean Museum Picture Library, University of Oxford, England.

Page 19. *Pan and Daphnis* by Heliodoros. Marble sculpture. Collezione Farnese, Naples. Photograph © BEBA/AISA. Courtesy the Bridgeman Art Library and Museo Archeologico Nazionale di Napoli, Italy.

Page 20. Erotic scene, Casa del Centenario (Villa of Centenary), Pompeii, Italy. Fresco. Photo: Fotografica Foglia. Photo Credit: Scala / Art Resource, NY.

Page 23. *Adam and Eve* by Albert Dürer. Engraving, 9.86 × 7.86 in. (25.1 × 20 cm). Courtesy the Bridgeman Art Library and the British Museum, London, England.

Pages 24–25. *The Sleeping Venus* by Giorgione. Oil on canvas, 42.7 × 68.9 in. (108.5 × 175 cm). © Staatliche Kunstsammlungen, Dresden, Germany. Courtesy the Bridgeman Art Library and Gemaeldegalerie Alte Meister, Dresden, Germany.

Page 26. *The Temptation of St. Anthony* by Veronese. Oil on canvas, 78 × 59.4 in. (198 × 151 cm). Courtesy the Bridgeman Art Library and Musee des Beaux-Arts, Caen, France.

Pages 28–29. *Leda and the Swan* by Michelangelo. Pen and ink on paper, 41.5 in. × 55.5 in. (105.4 × 141 cm). Courtesy the Bridgeman Art Library and the Musee des Beaux-Arts, Orleans, France, Giraudon.

Page 31. *Cupid and Psyche* by François Gérard. Oil on canvas. Courtesy the Bridgeman Art Library and the Louvre, Paris, France.

Page 32. *The Mysterious Rose Garden* by Aubrey Beardsley. Lithograph for *The Yellow Book*. Private collection. Photo © AISA. Courtesy the Bridgeman Art Library.

Page 33. Spine designs by Aubrey Beardsley for *The Yellow Book*, volumes II–XIII, published 1894–97. Courtesy the Stapleton Collection, the Bridgeman Art Library.

Pages 35–37. Color woodblock prints by Katsushika Hokusai. Courtesy the Bridgeman Art Library and the British Library, London, England.

Pages 40–41. *A Satyr Mourning Over a Nymph*, by Piero di Cosimo. Oil on panel. Courtesy the Bridgeman Art Library and the British Museum, London, England.

Pages 42–43. *Recumbent Nymph* by Anselm Feuerbach. Oil on canvas. Courtesy the Bridgeman Art Library and Germanisches National Museum, Nuremberg, Germany.

Page 45. *Venus and Cupid* by Lucas Cranach the Elder. Oil on panel. Courtesy the Bridgeman Art Library and Germanisches National Museum, Nuremberg, Germany.

Page 46. *The Three Graces* by Peter Paul Rubens. Oil on panel.

Courtesy the Bridgeman Art Library and Museo Nacional del Prado, Madrid, Spain.

Page 49. *Leda and the Swan* by Jacopo Rubusti Tintoretto. Oil on canvas, 63.78 × 85.83 in. (162 × 218 cm). Courtesy the Bridgeman Art Library and Galleria Degli Uffizi, Florence, Italy.

Page 51. *La Danaïde* by Auguste Rodin. Sculpture. Courtesy the Bridgeman Art Library and Musee Rodin, Paris, France.

Page 52. *Young Man Sitting by the Sea* by Jean-Hippolyte Flandrin. Oil on canvas. Courtesy the Bridgeman Art Library, © A. Dequier – M. Bard. Courtesy Louvre Museum, Paris, France.

Pages 54–55. Etchings from *Juliette* by Marquis (Donatien Alphonse François) de Sade.

Page 56. *The Origin of the World* by Gustave Courbet. Oil on canvas, 18.1 × 21.7 in. (46 × 55 cm). Courtesy the Bridgeman Art Library and Musee d'Orsay, Paris, France.

Page 59. *The Bed* by Henri de Toulouse-Lautrec. Oil on cardboard. Courtesy the Bridgeman Art Library and Musee d'Orsay, Paris, France.

Page 60. Plate from the *Lysistrata* by Aubrey Beardsley.

Page 62. *Wrestlers* by Thomas Eakins. Oil on canvas, 43.38 × 60 in. (122.87 × 152.4 cm). Photo © 2008 Museum Associates/ LACMA. Los Angeles County Museum of Art, Gift of Cecile C. Bartman and The Cecile and Fred Bartman Foundation.

Pages 64–65. *Tales from the Dressing Table* by Franz von Bayros.

Page 68. Film stills from *The Story of O* (*Histoire d'O*) based on the book by Pauline Reage (Anne Desclos). Courtesy the Everett Collection.

Pages 70–71. *Untitled* by Larry Clark. Black and white print,

11 × 14 in. (27.94 × 35.56 cm). Courtesy the artist and Luhring Augustine, New York, USA.

Page 72. *Collage* by William Curtis. Courtesy the artist.

Page 74. Vintage daguerreotype of French *fille de joie*, circa 1870. Courtesy private collection.

Page 75. Korova Milk Bar Waitress Uniform by Allen Jones. Sculpture. Courtesy Marlborough Fine Art, Ltd., London, England.

Pages 78–79. *Maissie in Yellow Panties* and *Gabby in the Kitchen* by Richard Kern. Photographs. Courtesy Feature, Inc., New York, USA.

Pages 82–83. *The Inconsistencies* by Matt Greene. Pencil on paper, 22 × 30 in. (55.9 × 76.2 cm). Courtesy Deitch Projects, New York, USA.

Page 85. *Pornokrates* by Felicien Rops. Pastel and gouache on paper. Courtesy the Musee Provincial Felicien Rops, Namur, Belgium. Photo Credit: Erich Lessing / Art Resource, NY.

Pages 86–87. *VB45* by Vanessa Beecroft. Kunsthalle Wien, Vienna, 2001. Photo: Armin Linke. Courtesy Vanessa Beecroft and Deitch Projects, New York, USA.

Page 88. *Untitled* by Terry Richardson. Photograph. Courtesy Trunk Archives, New York, USA.

ACKNOWLEDGMENTS

Dedicated to Melinda Gebbie.

With our appreciation for inspiration and support to: *Arthur*, John Coulthart, Francis Coy, Esther de Hollander, Neil Egan, Bernardo Guillermo, Eric Himmel, Michelle Ishay, Michael Jacobs, Charlie Kochman, Thurston Moore, Jutta Pakenis, Jacquie Poirier, Andrew Prinz, Barney Rosset, Kiki Sinclair, and Anet Sirna-Bruder.

Editor: Eva Prinz
Project Manager: Esther de Hollander
Production Manager: Jacquie Poirier

Library of Congress Cataloging-in-Publication Data

Moore, Alan, 1953-
25,000 years of erotic freedom / by Alan Moore.
p. cm.
ISBN 978-0-8109-4846-4 (Harry N. Abrams, Inc.)
1. Erotic art—History. 2. Pornography—History. I. Title. II. Title: Twenty-five thousand years of erotic freedom.

N8217.E6M66 2009
700'.453809—dc22

2009011821

Printed and bound in Hong Kong
10 9 8 7 6 5 4 3 2 1

Abrams books are available at special discounts when purchased in quantity for premiums and promotions as well as fundraising or educational use. Special editions can also be created to specification. For details, contact specialmarkets@abramsbooks.com or the address below.

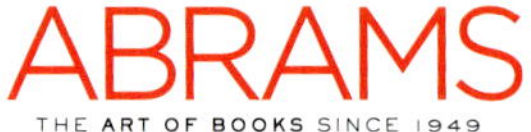

115 West 18th Street
New York, NY 10011
www.abramsbooks.com

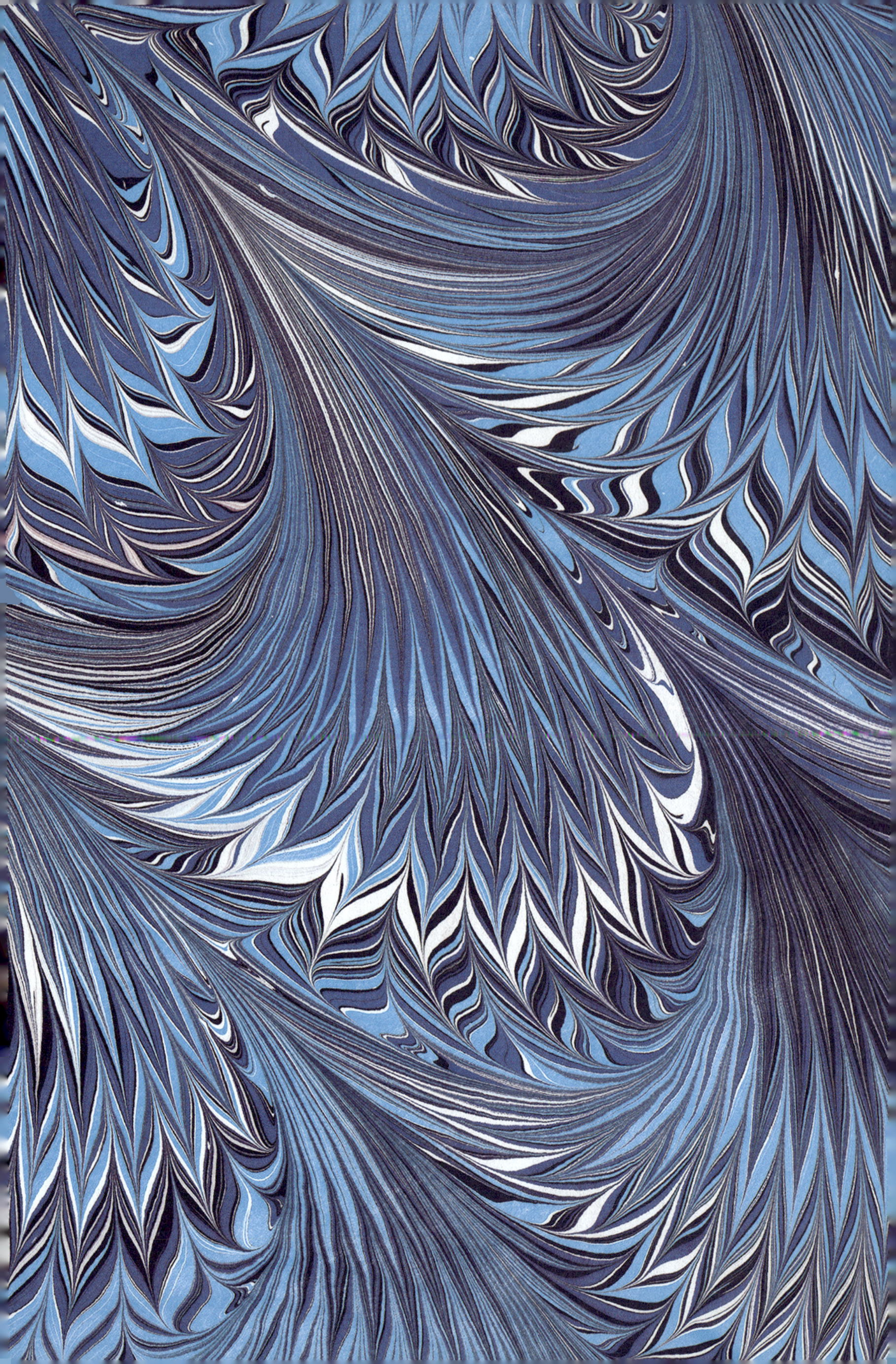